The Challenges
of the
Twenty-First-Century Church

SCOTT A. BRADLEY

ISBN 978-1-64079-739-0 (Paperback)
ISBN 978-1-64079-740-6 (Digital)

Copyright © 2017 by Scott A. Bradley
All rights reserved. No part of this publication may be reproduced, distributed, or transmitted in any form or by any means, including photocopying, recording, or other electronic or mechanical methods without the prior written permission of the publisher. For permission requests, solicit the publisher via the address below.

Christian Faith Publishing, Inc.
296 Chestnut Street
Meadville, PA 16335
www.christianfaithpublishing.com

Printed in the United States of America

Contents

Chapter 1: The Changing American Culture................7
Ministering to an Emerging Culture..........8
The Culture of Modern Thought...............9
Chapter 2: The Church without Principle..................11
Chapter 3: The Testimony of Christian Lifestyle........18
Chapter 4: The Lack of Equipment for Battle...........22
The Filling of the Holy Spirit 25
Chapter 5: The Electronic Church and
the Gospel of Prosperity...........................27
The Beggar and the Rich Man in
the Twenty-First-Century Church............30
Jesus's Challenge to
the Young Rich Ruler...............................32
Chapter 6: The Master-Servant Relationship.............35
Religious Arrogance..................................37
Chapter 7: The Twenty-First-Century Church:
The Great Compromise...........................41
The Intellectual Challenge........................44
The Fractured Teachings..........................45

	Silver-Tongued Orators..................46
Chapter 8:	The Megachurch 51
	The Persecution against the Church..........53
Chapter 9:	We're Dealing with This Kind...................56
	Jesus Warning about Demons 58
	Spiritual Rank................................59
	No Prayer Life 61
	Knowing the Master's Will....................62
	The Fasting Prayer 64
Chapter 10:	To Hell with 'Em................................66
Chapter 11:	The Twenty-First-Century Church and President Barack Obama...................72
	Obama and the Gay Agenda....................73
	Gay Rights vs. Civil Rights 75
Chapter 12:	The Emergence of Islam in America 82
	Islamic Indoctrination in America's Youth 83
	Who Is Allah? 84
	The Spread of Islam...........................87
	The Nation of Islam 89
	The Falsehood of Chrislam.....................93
Chapter 13:	New Age and Pantheism 97
Chapter 14:	The Relevance and Power of the True Gospel Message....................102

  Ministering to the Next Generation........104
  The Culture in the Hood......................105
  The Ministry of Jesus............................107
Chapter 15: What We Don't Know Hurts Us.............111
  Defending Who Jesus Is........................112
  The Historic Jesus.................................113
  The Validity of the Bible.......................115
  Defending the Triune God.....................117
  The Reality of Satan:
  the Enemy of God and Man...................120
Chapter 16: America: Blessed and Backslidden...........123

Chapter One

The Changing American Culture

Culture is defined as the ethics, philosophy, and traditions of a society. It is, by and large, the way of life that establishes customs and overall laws written as well as unwritten and, therefore, assumed and observed by the society. The culture is usually established by religious observations and commandments.

American culture has observed biblical principle since its inception, and its Constitution and laws were founded upon biblical laws. Although the American Constitution guarantees freedom of speech and religion, it was still founded upon Christian principles. The Bible is used in the court systems and in Congress. Whenever a new president is inaugurated and takes the oath of office, he places his hand on the Bible.

Although there is an American culture, it is impossible to say that America has only one culture as there are many cultures within the main culture itself. After all, American prides herself in being called the great melting pot, a variance, and combining all cultures from around the world.

Some have evolved, assimilated, and are shared among each other.

Ministering to an Emerging Culture

Although cultures change with time, the traditional American culture has greatly changed within the past fifty years. Generations are associated with and even defined by their signature, which often leaves an imprint or impression to the overall society. These generations contribute to the lingo, arts, and attitudes that, in some cases, have even changed the culture itself.

The attitudes of morality are slowly fading from society that we are living in as biblical standards are being forsaken for "modern thought." One of the reasons has to do with the rebellion of the '70s. During this era, the youth had rebelled against the establishment, coining phrases like, "Do your thing," "If it feels good, do it," and "Let it all hang out!" They took on such monikers as "hippies, beatniks, and flower children." They rebelled against the "Establishment," particularly because of the Viet Nam War that was raging at the time and felt that the direction being taken by the country was leading them to destruction. Although history has proven that America's involvement in Viet Nam was a mistake, it was a contributing factor to changing attitudes in the American culture.

The Culture of Modern Thought

There was a term used to describe that era called the Generation Gap. This in short meant that the younger generation was not only rejecting the wisdom of the previous, but looking at them as enemies of the advancement of the culture. It was also defined by "free love" and "free sex," with less emphasis of the sacred institute of marriage along with the elimination of what otherwise was shameful behavior. However, it was just a matter of time until that generation of hippies, beatniks, and flower children grew up and became a part of the current decision-making society. The phrases of the '70s became the standard of the current generation. Hence, the attitude of the culture changed, reflecting the rebellion of the people. "If it feels good, do it," "Let it all hang out," and "Do your thing!" was no longer what they *said* in the '70s, but what they *do* in the present. It is therefore easier for this culture to accept things such as premarital sex, abortion, homosexuality, and common-law marriages.

One of the great challenges to twenty-first-century ministry is dealing with a society where *shame* is nonexistent. Whereas at one time it was taboo to live in common-law marriage or for a young lady to become pregnant out of wedlock, the attitude of the culture now accepts this as normal and even encourages it with new terms like "my baby's momma" or "my baby's daddy," as if to disconnect oneself from the father or mother. Homosexuality, when at one time was looked down upon, now has the endorsement from the highest office in the country—the president of the United States—and there are now openly gay churches.

Political Correctness is now more important to the culture than the Bible and Christian principles. In fact, Christianity in the minds of many is outdated, and much of the upcoming generations are exploring new religions and new philosophies. So the challenges to Christianity are greater because the American culture is changing.

Therefore, one of the first things that one must understand in Christian ministry is that the twenty-first-century American culture is offended by traditional Christianity, and the minister must be aware now more than ever that his message may not be readily accepted. He may face challenges from other religions, particularly with the rise of other religious ideas and philosophies and even among traditional Christian churches that are compromising for political correctness for fear of repercussions.

Chapter Two

The Church without Principle

Another problem of the twenty-first-century church is the lack of principle or conviction, meaning living a life that reflects Christ. People have forgotten Christ's purpose for His church. First John 2:15-16 says,

> *Love not the world, neither the things that are in the world. If any man love the world the love of the Father is not in him.*
>
> *For all that is in the world, the lust of the flesh, and the lust of the eyes, and the pride of life, is not of the Father, but of the world.*

It is true that we are in the world and must abide by the world system. But our first love should be of the *world* to come. I often say that we are passing through *time* but destined for *eternity*, and therefore, we understand that anything we encounter, gain, or lose in this world is temporary. Placing love for temporary things is not wise because it can be lost while we are yet in the world. Jesus said to build your treasures in heaven.

> *For where your treasure is, there will your heart be also. (Matt. 6:19-20)*

Principle in the life of the believer first comes when Jesus becomes Lord. It reflects the attitude that one has toward Christ and the people they are ministering to. There are many professing Christians who wear the title and attend church, but Jesus is not the Lord of their life. Lord means *master*, and we are the *servant*. The motive of the servant is to *first* please his master. The first conviction is to follow the will of the Lord even if it means denying our own will. *"If any man will come after me, let him deny himself, and take up his cross daily, and follow me"* (Luke 9:23).

Apostle Paul asked the question, *"Shall we continue in sin; that grace may abound? God forbid. How shall we that are dead to sin, continue any longer therein?" (Rom. 6:1-2).*

Sinning against the master should bring conviction as well as repentance. Not because one was caught, but because one realizes that sin has offended his master. Unfortunately, many professing Christians have no such relationship and therefore have no principle about living unrepentant with practiced sin.

As we have move in to the twenty-first century, the influence of the church over the past twenty-five years has lost its influence, particularly on the American culture and the overall thinking of people in general. The morality of common sense seems to have been lost in selfish and self-centered ideas motivated by pleasures and what the Bible describes as a generation who are *"lovers of their own selves...lovers of pleasure, more than lovers of God"* (2 Tim. 3:2, 4).

Sexuality and the sacredness of the God-ordained institution of marriage are becoming obsolete. Common-law marriage, fornication, adultery, pornography, and homosexuality are common. Because there is no conviction from the pulpits, people who practice these things feel no need to repent or turn away from these sins. No one wants to say that things are wrong for fear of backlash.

This is why when at one time people didn't feel comfortable living this way, they now can walk into any church and settle in. If they come to a church where these things are addressed, they accuse the church of being a place of hatred.

Certainly, the high-profile celebrity televangelist will not address these issues for fear of losing their celebrity status and donations. They fear they will be called hate preachers, bigots, out of step, or even losing their tax-exempt status. Instead, they will only preach motivational sermons. There is no conviction from many of the high-profile celebrity preachers.

The spread of first century Christianity was through preaching and fellowship among all nations. On the day of Pentecost, Saint Peter preached, and three thousand souls were baptized, thus the beginning of Christ's church. And because of the fervency of their preaching, they were called *Christians*.

I am reminded of a Sunday morning sermon I heard that discussed the possibility of life on Mars, or the one where the minister discussed recipes for Christmas dinner. Imagine if someone had attended the church for the first time and was seeking answers to questions they had about God. Unless *they* were an astronomer or a cook, they would have left those services disappointed.

Because of the lack of conviction or true faith in the Bible as God's holy word, the church has become a social center with current topics discussed and motivational speech to make the congregation feel good about themselves and life, not warning them that the wages of sin is *still* death, and that although God is a God of love, He still holds us accountable for unrepentant or continued practice of sin. Many of the churches are no longer Bible-centered, and therefore, the attendees have never made a commitment to Christ.

The early church spent much time in prayer and fasting and did not compromise their faith in Jesus, proclaiming to the world that He is the *only* hope of mankind. This is in contrast to the church today as many Christian leaders are compromising the faith and even incorporating teachings of other religions into Christian theology, trying to find common ground and even accepting the idea that God is in all religions. One famous entertainment celebrity going as far as to say, "We all worship the same god, we just call him different names." This, of course, is a direct contradiction to what Jesus said when He stated, *"No man comes to the father except by me"* (John 14:6).

The preaching of the Gospel must be done with conviction, influenced by the Holy Spirit of God, with an uncompromising fervor. God's Word is right. There is no other alternative. When Jesus said, *"I am the way, the truth, and the life; no man cometh to the Father, but by me"* (John 14:6), the twenty-first-century American culture would tag this *politically incorrect*. All major religions are challenged. If Jesus said He is the only *way*, then Buddha, Mohammed, and all others are false teachers with a false hope. Yet the boldness and directness of this statement clearly shows that *He* alone is the only way to heaven, and that all other ways, no matter how sincere or popular among the masses, are in error. He is not *showing* the way; He *is* the way. He is not just *telling* the truth; He is *truth* incarnated. He is not just *giving* life. Life is nonexistent except *in Him*.

The early church was also persecuted for spreading the Gospel as many of them were beaten, imprisoned, and slaughtered. Of the twelve Apostles, which include Matthias, who replaced Judas, all of them died as a martyr except for Saint John—the only one to die of natural causes, but not without persecutions.

The reality is that the church in the twenty-first century is getting smaller. It is because of the lack of conviction from the pulpits that laity has become lackadaisical, disgusted, or unconcerned. Apostle Paul warned us that in the last days, there would be a great falling away from the faith (2 Thess. 2:3). Even though people still attend church, the conviction of living a godly lifestyle or sharing the faith with others has taken a back seat to self-pleasure and personal agenda. The message from the American pulpits is no longer Bible-centered. Jesus is not the center of attraction. The church has become a social club, a fashion show, a hot spot. It feels the need to incorporate entertainment into its service to hold the interest of the people. No one is challenged to live a godly and principled lifestyle.

Jesus said, *"Ye are the salt of the earth. But if the salt has lost its saviour…it is therefore good for nothing"* (Matt. 5:13). Therefore, if the church loses its purpose and power, there will be a great spoil amid the surroundings as evident in today's society. In recent years, the European church has experienced this as many are turning from Christianity, and hundreds of churches are closing.

It appears that church scandals are on the rise, and although there have always been scandals, the electronic media exposes more high-profile leaders complete with details of names, places, and times. After being exposed, there appears to be more self-justification and explanations rather than repentance. In fact, it seems that most are sorry because they were caught and not because they were wrong. This is not just from the high-profile celebrity preachers, but even among lay members. If there is no principle from the pulpits, there certainly will be none among the lay members. It also contributes to the fact that no one wants to admit that they are wrong. When it is justifiable in the church, everyone feels justified, no matter how wrong they are. This also gives way for ungodly things into the society at large.

Chapter Three

The Testimony of Christian Lifestyle

I have a personal saying that I believe is biblical base. And that is "I do not live right *to be saved*. I live right *because I'm saved.*" The servant emulates his master, and therefore, the lifestyle of a Christian should reflect the one whom he follows. I've even heard it said that the greatest testimony one could have is the life they live. The songwriter penned lyrics that said, *"Let the life you live be a reflection of the man inside."*

That being said, there is still the mistake that many people make, that heaven is earned by being good or that we can *earn* salvation. This only leads people being judgmental toward another because of how one may keep the rules better than others. We must remember that we are saved by grace and not by works. But notice the words of Apostle Paul: *"Shall we continue in sin that grace may abound? God forbid. How shall we that are dead to sin, continue any longer therein?"* (Rom. 6:1-2).

The true born-again Christian hates sin because it is an offense to our Lord and, therefore, should avoid sinning.

This does not mean that we will not sin, but that we should not willfully practice it. In this verse, Apostle Paul acknowledges the grace of God, but that if we are true followers of Him, we should not be willing participants in sin.

The first impression that the world sees of the Christian is the lifestyle that would identify them as such. Apostle Paul says, *"Ye are our epistle written in our hearts, known and read of men"* (2 Cor. 3:2). People may *read* you before they read the Bible. They may observe a professing Christian before they attend a church. You become the advertisement for the product; in this case, the product is the gospel of Christ.

I have found it *disturbing* when I hear entertainers who are about to receive music or video awards, which usually are full of profanity and sexual explicitness, give "their Lord and savior Jesus Christ praise for this award." Would Christ approve of such profanity-laced lyrics or be glorified by songs about fornication? It makes me wonder who they have sat under to learn about Jesus as they can be a reflection of the failure of ministry.

The term *Christian* was not originally used by the early followers of Jesus, but was a label given to believers by the world because they were followers of Christ (Acts 11:26). They were identified by their lifestyle, the way they talked, the way they lived, what they did not partake in or rebuffed.

This is not to say that Christians do not make mistakes, have weaknesses and flaws, but that by being a follower of Christ, we walk in humility and not arrogance.

I recall when I served in the United States Marine Corps in the '80s, there was a fellow Marine who was from my hometown of Chicago. He didn't really stand out to me much because he acted like most of our fellow Marines, cursing, telling nasty jokes, and passing around pornographic material.

I did not do those things because I was taught that Christians do not do such things. But secondly, I felt that if I was to have a true testimony to those around me, I had to present myself differently, having a conviction of my beliefs by my lifestyle. I also knew that to present myself arrogantly before them would make me look as though I was "holier than thou," hence making my testimony of none affect. So I socialized with them, laughed and talked, but I always kept my convictions and shared my faith. Some laughed and mocked me, but others showed respect and allowed me to share my faith with them.

One morning as I walked by the brother from Chicago's bed (we called them racks), I noticed he was listening to one of my favorite gospel artists on his music player. I stopped and told him I recognized the artist, and we began to talk. I found out that not only was he professing to be saved, but that he was also a minister. Much to his credit, afterward, he got himself together, stopped cursing, and no longer participated in passing around pornography among the troops, and we became good friends. We even started preaching together at one of the local churches.

But his lifestyle before his fellow Marines had damaged his credibility, especially since he never confessed to falling into weakness but continued to insist that he was always saved, even during his time of profanity and pornography.

Again I am not judging him, for who among us has not had weak moments of even weak periods, especially since we were away from home and the influence of the church. And although the Lord will forgive us as we continue to walk in His grace, our lifestyle can destroy our testimony.

I am also reminded of when I played basketball in one of our church league games. We held to church tradition by having prayer on the court before each game, usually led by me. This particular game became very competitive, and during the course of it, a scuffle broke out with one of the players yelling a profane word at the other.

"I guess that prayer didn't do no good!" the ref said. And hence in his eyes, at least, the credibility of the whole church league was under hypocrisy.

Let me reemphasize that moments of weakness do not disqualify one from being saved, and who among us has not had them? What I am saying is that it is at those moments that people will judge us, and arrogance rather than humility will keep us unfavorable in their eyes.

Chapter Four

The Lack of Equipment for Battle

> No wise person goes in to battle without being properly equipped. Those that are not soon become casualties. Apostle Paul warned us that we are in a spiritual battle.
> —Ephesians 6:11, 2 Corinthians 10:4

Unfortunately, many twenty-first-century Christians are ignorant, not only to the devices of Satan, but many don't believe in his existence. The "prosperity gospel" has caused many to change focus to the natural and negligent of the spiritual.

Whereas previous generations identified the devil trying to resist him, this generation calls it superstition and attributes things to coincidence or emotional disorders. Many twenty-first-century Christians don't read or know the Bible, relying instead on the minister or teacher to teach them, never checking or following up to know for oneself.

THE CHALLENGES OF THE TWENTY-FIRST-CENTURY CHURCH

Some disturbing statistics show that many don't know common biblical stories because they have either never been taught or never sat long enough under biblical teachings to learn. A recent study reveal:

Christians claim to believe the Bible is God's Word. We claim it's God's divinely inspired, inerrant message to us. Yet despite this, we aren't reading it. A recent Life Way Research study found only 45 percent of those who regularly attend church read the Bible more than once a week. Over 40 percent of the people attending read their Bible occasionally, maybe once or twice a month. Almost 1 in 5 churchgoers say they never read the Bible—essentially the same number who read it every day.

Because we don't read God's Word, it follows that we don't know it. To understand the effects, we can look to statistics of another Western country: the United Kingdom. The United Kingdom Bible Society surveyed British children and found many could not identify common Bible stories. When given a list of stories, almost 1 in 3 didn't choose the Nativity as part of the Bible and over half (59 percent) didn't know that Jonah being swallowed by the great fish is in the Bible.

British parents didn't do much better. Around 30 percent of parents don't know Adam and Eve,

David and Goliath, or the Good Samaritan are in the Bible. To make matters worse, 27 percent think Superman is or might be a biblical story. More than 1 in 3 believes the same about Harry Potter. And more than half (54 percent) believe The Hunger Games is or might be a story from the Bible... There is little excuse for anyone living in Western Civilization, particularly Christians, to not know or read the Bible. Nine out of ten American homes have at least one Bible. The average American—Christian or not—owns at least three Bibles. And technology has put Bibles at our fingertips wherever we are—you can download the Bible for free on your smartphone.[1]

The Scriptures says, *"My people are destroyed for lack of knowledge"* (Hosea 4:6). Knowledge is obtainable through study. The lack of it keeps one in ignorance.

Because of the lack of knowledge of the Bible, it becomes easier for one to be deceived, hence, the rise of cultism and Christians buying into other religions because they do not know how to define their faith.

---

[1] Read more at http://www.prophecynewswatch.com/2015/July14/145.html#2QKoLsFkkBAm2Dsm.99.

The Filling of the Holy Spirit

Apostle Paul said, *"Be not drunken with wine...but be filled with the Spirit"* (Eph. 5:18). Jesus commanded the church to wait for the promise of the Holy Spirit, *"and ye shall be witnesses unto me"* (Acts 1:8).

One of the attributes of the Holy Spirit within the believer is the power to live holy. Being filled with the Spirit enables one to live holy. He gives conviction to help one live a godly lifestyle, anoints one to preach and teach the gospel, gives us power over Satan, and He comforts us.

It was through the Holy Spirit that gave the first-century church boldness to proclaim Jesus as Christ to a nonbelieving world and against opposition.

Whereas Saint Peter denied Christ on the night of His passion for fear of the retribution, after He was filled with the Holy Spirit, he boldly preached Christ on the day of Pentecost.

After the persecution of the church in weeks that follow, the Bible says they came together and asked God for more boldness:

> *And now, Lord, behold their threatenings: and grant unto thy servants, that with all boldness they may speak they word,,, And when they had prayed, the place was shaken where they were assembled together; and they were filled with the Holy Ghost, and they spake the word of God with boldness. (Acts 4:29, 31)*

Boldness is what the twenty-first-century church needs as its voice has gone silent in the face of opposition for fear of consequence. Not only has it gone silent, in many cases it has compromised with ungodly attitudes of the world for fear of being called politically incorrect, being placed on a hate list, being isolated, verbally attacked, or even losing tax-exempt status.

The first-century church feared no such retributions, even rejoicing when they were beaten and threatened not to preach in the name of Jesus by the religious leaders of that day (Acts 5:41).

Note the words of Saint Peter in the face of threatening of persecution: "We ought to obey God rather than men" (Acts 5:29).

Chapter Five

The Electronic Church and the Gospel of Prosperity

The twentieth century saw a number of technological advancements and breakthroughs, which included medical advancements as well. In fact, mankind has accomplished more inventive ways in the last hundred years than he has in all of his existence on the planet. A hundred years ago, there were no televisions, cell phones, computers, or Internet. Yet one hundred years later, we practically cannot live without them as they have become intertwined in our everyday lives.

Whereas at one time people attended church because it was part of the American culture, nowadays I have noticed that getting people to come to church and attend services often centers around what is on TV. The electronic media, which came into existence in the twentieth century, has had a great impact on the American culture. It not only influences the thought process of the culture, but it has also created a competition for the attention of the people.

The twenty-first-century American church is in competition with sports, reality TV, concerts, musicals, and entertainment TV. In fact, many televangelists (a new word to describe the TV preachers and their churches) have taken advantage of this media and are preaching via satellite, cable, and internet to take the gospel message throughout the world. Souls can be reached anywhere in the world, which before the invention of this media was impossible. A minister cannot always judge the impact of his ministry by the size of his congregation if he has access to this media as he can preach to an audience in cyberspace that he may never see or meet. You would think that these are the best tools to preach the gospel to the entire world.

Because of this technology, a man can be heard by the masses long after he has died via CDs and DVDs. I personally attended a funeral service where the deceased literally preached at his own funeral via a DVD and a projector screen while his body lay stretched out before the altar. It was like he was dead and alive in the same room at the same time.

Some of the televangelist mastered the look for media, attired in fine colorful suits and shimmering diamonds, very camera friendly. There is, however, an apparent change in the message of some. The electronic church, which, although is an excellent means of reaching the masses, the twenty-first-century message has become a mixture of prosperity, self-service compromise, and what being *blessed* is supposedly all about.

The Bible-believing gospel preacher has been replaced by the motivational speaker with the principles of better living and positives attitudes. The message of salvation and eternal hope in Christ has been replaced by prosperity and riches.

This message has presented Jesus as this Santa Claus-like figure who rewards His children with "blessings" for their faithfulness to the televangelist by sending "seed" offerings, which in turn help him stay on TV and finances his mansions, Mercedes Benz, and personal jets. In fact, because of these types of ministries, people judge a *blessed* person by how much they have. A man with a nice car is considered blessed, while a man with a not-so-nice car needs *more faith*. Some of the televangelists, for fear of losing ratings, popularity, and receiving the *seeds* compromised, choose to remain politically correct and not offend anyone by preaching against sin. The gospel preacher who cries out against sin and stands firmly on the Bible is considered outdated and a hate preacher.

I am a firm believer that the Lord does bless, heal, and deliver and have experienced it in my life as well as in my ministry. However, I think that it is important to understand that "blessings" are not just finance and substances like new cars, houses, and clothes. Further, it appears that these "blessings" only apply to the rich American cultures as opposed to those who live in oppressed countries. Like Lazarus the beggar in the Bible, they would be satisfied with scrapes from the tables of the rich (Luke 16:20-21).

Lost in the messages of prosperity is the fact that the Lord wants first place in our lives (Matt. 6:33) and that there is more than blessing of finance and wealth. Many of the people who followed Jesus did not follow Him for the miracles and the preaching, but for the fishes and loaves (John 6:26-27). In other words, they followed Jesus because they got free fish sandwiches. When He stopped supplying the sandwiches, the people stopped following Him (John 6:66). The same can be said today that many are following Jesus because of the hope of prospering with new things like cars, homes, and money preached by the "prosperity preaching" or the televangelist. They have learned to love the things but not the one who has provided the things.

Third John 2 says, *"Beloved, I wish above all things that thou mayest prosper and be in health, even as thy soul prosper."* He's speaking of being holistic, financial, physical, and spiritual. All these things are gained by *working* toward them. They do not just drop out of the sky. Physical health does not just happen. It is gained by exercise and healthy eating. Spiritual prosperity is gained through prayer, fasting, and reading God's Word. Commitment and consistency is the key to spiritual growth. Prosperity of any kind comes with time, effort, and hard work.

The Beggar and the Rich Man in the Twenty-First-Century Church

Jesus told a story of a rich man and Lazarus (Luke 16:19-31). Lazarus was a poor, sick beggar. By some of today's preachers' standards, he was not blessed. He did not have a victorious testimony of riches and wealth. He did not have a miracle of healing; in fact, he was sick. He had no "seed offering" to invest in anyone's ministry. He was probably gaunt from starvation and only desired the table scraps from the rich man's table. If this man had walked into the twenty-first-century church, he would have been shunned by the people. His begging would have been irritating. It reminds me of the minister who said on TV, "I don't want any poor or poverty-stricken people attending this church!"

I have seen this happen on numerous occasions where such persons have come into churches, asking for something to eat, only to be ignored or pushed aside. Lazarus visits our churches often and usually is treated the same way that the rich man treated him in Jesus's story.

Let's look at this rich man. Because he was wealthy, by today's standards he was "blessed." If he lived in this day, he would have driven the finest of cars, lived in a nice home, possibly a mansion. He would have had political influence, dressed in the best suits and shoes. No one would know nor would anyone want to know how he came about his wealth, just how much was he going to donate to the ministry. Although this man was the more desirable of the two, the Bible says that when he died, he went to hell and is eternally tormented in the flames of it. Yet Lazarus, the poor beggar whom everyone shunned, received an angelic escort to the bosom of Abraham.

The twenty-first-century church would place the rich man in heaven simply because of the way he looked to the people: prosperous and progressive. It did not matter that he didn't live according to God's standards, had arrogance that people today call self-confidence, or that he had no compassion for those of lesser status. At his funeral, he would have been praised as a great humanitarian and contributor to charitable causes. Yet nothing anyone said would determine his eternal destiny. Man looks on the outward appearance, but God knows the heart (1 Sam. 16:7).

Jesus's Challenge to the Young Rich Ruler

Saint Matthew 19:16-25 tells of a young rich ruler who came to Jesus and asked, *"What good thing shall I do that I may have eternal life?"* The question is typical of all religions that mistakably think that heaven and eternal life are gained by good works. Apostle Paul later tells us that heavens is not gained by works, but by *grace* (Eph. 2:8-9).

Jesus, knowing all things, responded with a religious answer: *"Keep the commandments."*

"Which?" the man asked.

Jesus knew the man's heart and further engaged him by naming the specific commandments. The young man told Jesus that he was an observer of the commandments since his youth. *"What lack I yet?"*

It was at this moment that Jesus challenged him with something that was close to him: his wealth. It should be understood that wealth is not a sin, but in the case of this young man, it had become his *god.* Anything in our lives that the Lord cannot have, or take, or that we place *before* our God has placed Him second in our lives and therefore becomes sin. People will love and worship the blessing, but ignore the one who has blessed them.

Jesus knew the heart of the man, and even though he was morally good and was an observer of the laws of God, his true *god* was his wealth. This can be a problem in anyone's life, and the hindrance can become anything that we place ahead of God.

I think about the man I knew who, while in church service one Sunday, had his car broken into. From that point on, he continued to come *to* church faithfully but, for fear of it happening again, would send his family into the church while he remained in his car in the parking lot during the service. This man's priorities placed his car ahead of God.

Family, friends, home, and cars can all become *gods* if they take priority over the true and living God. Jesus said, *"Seek ye first the kingdom of God and His righteousness, and all of these things shall be added unto you"* (Matt. 6:33). The motive of the servants is to *first* seek the will of his master.

Jesus spoke of how hard it was for a rich man to enter the kingdom. This is because of a basic principle. The more one has, the less one wants to give up. Yet this young man would be a model figure for the "blessed man" of the twenty-first century, even though he had just rejected Jesus in favor of his wealth.

In contrast, there was another rich man named Zacchaeus, and unlike the young rich man who was a beloved ruler, he was short in stature and despised by the people because he was a tax collector and had a reputation for gaining his wealth by dishonest means. When Jesus saw him, He invited Himself to Zacchaeus's house:

Zacchaeus, make haste, and come down; for today I must abide at thy house. (Luke 19:5)

Because of his encounter with Jesus, everything else, including his wealth, had become secondary. He was so honored that Jesus would recognize him and eat at his home that he freely volunteered to redistribute his wealth and reconcile anyone that he had cheated. Jesus said, *"This day is salvation come into this house."*

Zacchaeus had a change of heart. Jesus had become his priority and, unlike the young rich ruler, was willing to share his wealth.

Chapter Six

The Master-Servant Relationship

Slavery is offensive to the culture in the western hemisphere and particularly among African-Americans as many of our ancestry suffered the horrors and injustices of American slavery.

Slavery, however, is not exclusive among the American culture and has at one time or another been a part of all cultures and nations throughout time around the world. Some Africans were enslaved by others before coming to American.

All slave systems throughout time were not the same. Some were Prisoners of War (POW) as a result of tribal wars or wars among nations. Some cultures had a system of slavery designs to repay debts. This was the type of slavery during biblical times in the ancient Jewish culture. There were basically three types of slaves: the bond servant, the free-servant, and the hired servant.

The *hired* servant was basically an employee who had no benefit outside of his employment to the master. This was the attitude of the prodigal son who had wasted his inheritance and now suffered the consequence. He was starving and broke and thought about the employees of his father who had more than enough food. The young man was repentant and didn't come home with arrogance but humility to simply ask his father for a job as a hired servant (Luke 15:11-19).

The *bond* servant was indebted for a period of time to pay off his debt to the master, usually for a period of seven years. Sometimes this type of servitude required the entire family. It was this type of slave system that Apostle Paul admonished the servants to obey their masters (Eph. 6:5) and not the type of cruel, unjust, demeaning, and destructive system African-Americans experienced.

In the ancient Jewish culture, a slave could be sold in the event that the master owed another and therefore sold his slaves. The breaking up of the family in this case, however, was illegal, and families could not be broken up except under dire circumstances.

The *free*-servant was a person who, after his years of bond servitude, freely desired to stay in the debt of his master. He may have lived better as a servant and loved the family. The gesture of this was for the servant to pierce his ear with a gold earring, indicating a free-will bondage to his master. He would have benefited as the rest of the family, lived on the estate, and in some cases received and inheritance.

It is this type of servitude, the *free-servant,* that the Christian is to his master Jesus Christ as we are freely indebted to Him. Because we love Him, our motive is to do His will.

Religious Arrogance

I sat in a revival service, and the evangelist told everyone, *"Point your finger toward heaven and say, 'Lord, give me everything I deserve!'"* She then proceeded to tell everyone we *deserve* God's best. This is one of the moments in my life where I thank God He *didn't* answer prayer.

The reality is if God were to give us what we *deserve*, we'd all be in hell right now! The arrogance of the twenty-first-century church is prompted by the idea that we *deserve* the Lord's blessings, forgetting that when we are blessed, it is because He is good to us and not that we are good. This arrogance even makes one feel more blessed than another because he has obtained more "blessings" than someone else. This is not the attitude of a servant.

It should also be understood that the servant understands the consequence for disobedience. Again, this is something strongly lacking in the modern message of the prosperity preacher. The idea of *deserving* good things seems to be one-sided in that if one deserves good things, shouldn't one deserve punishment for disobedience? If one can point his finger toward the heavens and arrogantly demand what they deserve, what makes one think that they deserve good things in the first place?

Apostle Paul reminds us:

For by grace are ye saved through faith; and not that of yourselves: it is the gift of God, Not by works, lest any man should boast. (Eph. 2:8-9)

Because we are the recipients of the grace of God and because we have free will, we voluntarily serve Him. We cannot boast that we are good enough to be saved or are deserving of His salvation; it is strictly and exclusively His grace.

A servant attitude is humility, recognizing that the master is greater. We sometimes forget that we are servants of the Lord and stewards over what He has given us. He is not a mythological Santa Claus figure just giving gifts for good behavior. He is Lord/Master. The motive of the servant is to please his master, seek the will of his master, and carry out the wishes of his master. He responds to the command of his master and does not make demands upon him.

Both Moses and David, though esteemed high in the minds of people, were still servants, and their disobedience cost them dearly. Moses was not allowed to enter into the Promised Land (Num. 20:11-12). King David, who was called a man after God's heart, also suffered the consequence because of his disobedience (2 Sam. 12:1-23). In both cases, it was simply the servant rebelling against the will of the master because the servant's will took priority over the master's.

The humility of servitude also means that one accepts the place where the master has placed him. In the master's house, some were placed in honorable positions and some in less honorable positions. Some were stewards over much, some not as much. Jesus told the parable of the master who called together three servants and gave them charge over a portion of his wealth (Matt. 25:15-30). He did not give every servant the same amount and, therefore, did not judge them by what he had given to another. Every man was judged by his ability and what he had received. Jesus said, *"For unto whomsoever much is given, of him shall be much is required"* (Luke 12:48).

The servant with the larger amount of talents would have had no right to judge the man with less. After all, it all belonged to the master. The servant with less had no right to look upon the one with more and make excuse because he didn't have as much.

When the master returned to settle with his servants, he judged them the same but did not require the same amount, but according to what he distributed to them.

The first two servants took what they had and invested it and made returns, doubling their investments. The third servant took his master's money and buried it in the ground. Upon the master's return, he presented it to him just as he gave it to him. The first two servants were commended for their efforts and promoted within his kingdom.

The third servant was reprimanded by the master as being wicked and slothful, eventually casting him out of his kingdom because of his lack of action. I can imagine the servant's attitude when he was distributed only one talent; perhaps fearing his master, he did not want to touch it for fear of being accused a thief or even jealous of his fellow servants for not receiving as much, so he did nothing. It was his negligence that angered his lord.

As servants of the Lord, we are expected to take what talents, gifts, and abilities that He has given us and be productive. Many, however, are like the last servant—quiet, silent, nonproductive because we are afraid, ashamed, or feel like we do not have enough. But note what the master said to the servant that he was pleased with:

> *You have been faithful over a few things, I will make you ruler over many things. (Matt. 25:21)*

Note what caused their promotions: *"faithful over a few things."* Unfortunately, many Christians want promotions and blessings, but have not proven themselves faithful in small things. Like any employer, the Lord is not going to promote one who cannot be *trusted* with smaller tasks.

Chapter Seven

The Twenty-First-Century Church: The Great Compromise

Apostle Paul warned the Galatian church about those that would *pervert* the gospel or preach *another* (Gal. 1:6-9).

But though we, or an angel from heaven, preach any other gospel unto you than that which we have preached unto you, let him be accursed. (Gal. 1:8)

This would mean that all other religions and philosophies, though politically incorrect to say, are cursed. This is the harsh reality that Christians must face. But to reject this means that the consequences are dire as we reject the *true gospel* to take on a cursed teaching.

Because the true gospel teachings become *perverted*, it becomes easier for false teaching to be intertwined with biblical teachings. The idea of finding common ground among all religions may make sense in politics, hence politically correct, but it compromises true faith in Jesus Christ.

Cults that were one time isolated to their certain territories are now able to spread their doctrines across the world.

With the modern technology has also come modern philosophy that has not only interacted with religion, but has appealed to many high-profile entertainers who have a TV platform and, hence, can help spread this "newfound" religious philosophy.

True Christians, that is to say, those who have a servant-master relationship with Jesus Christ, are not easily moved, but it is the religious and even nonreligious that may follow what appears to make sense.

After the famous golfer Tiger Woods's confession of adulterous liaisons brought him before the national TV cameras to apologize, he stated that he was a Buddhist and would renew his faith and return to the religion of his upbringing.

I was in a department store watching the press conference on a large TV when a man standing next to me said, "He seems real sincere." Then he asked me, "Do you think he'll ever get back to where he was before all of this?"

"I hope so" I replied, as I have always been a fan of Tiger Woods

Then the man, not knowing me, said something else. "This woman said he needs Jesus! He doesn't need Jesus! He just said he was a Buddhist. People should stop forcing their religion on everybody."

Unfortunately, this man's philosophy is common as many feel that all religions are the same, even among professing Christians. Even a popular talk show host has stated that there are "many paths to God."

What many people don't understand, however, is that this philosophy is a direct challenge to what Jesus said: *"No man cometh to the Father, [except] by me"* (John 14:6).

To say that there are *many* paths to God when Jesus said, "I am the *only* way" is to call Jesus a liar, and therefore, those who profess to be Christians but believe that there are other paths to God are not true Christians.

Jesus asked His disciples, *"Whom do men say that I am?* (Matt. 16:13). He did not ask this question because He was concerned with popular opinion or what people necessarily thought of Him, but the questions had a deeper purpose. He was about to reveal Himself to the world as to who He was and His purpose. The response was similar to what religions say about Jesus today—a prophet, one of the prophets of old, the great teacher. If you asked the major religions today who Jesus was, they'd all say similar things: prophet, messenger, teacher, the reincarnation of an older prophet.

"But whom say ye that I am?" is the question He posed to his disciples. The response of Peter was deeper than religion. It was greater than what religion could ever do. The response was a revelation inspired by God Himself. *"Thou art the Christ, the Son of the living God."* Every religion does not believe or teach it. Even within Christianity, there are certain organizations, denominations, and cults that deny this. Jesus said, *"Upon this rock I will build my Church."* The *"Rock"* was not Peter, but the *revelation* that Peter received

from God, that *"Jesus is the Christ."* Although there are many that fall under the religious category of Christianity, not believing that Jesus is the Christ means that they are not a part of the *Church.* Many are religious, belong to an organization, even acknowledge Jesus one way or another, but are not part of the *Church.*

Unfortunately, there are many high-profile Christian ministers who have bought into the "New Age" philosophy and are forsaking the true gospel of Jesus Christ for a new-age compromise.

The Intellectual Challenge

One of Satan's strengths is his ability to appeal to mankind's intellect and therefore make perfect sense in what he says. One must stop and think that if Lucifer could convince one-third of the angels of heaven to rebel against God, or convince Adam and Eve in paradise to disobey God, or even to cause Judas, who was with Jesus, to betray Him, then it is obvious that he has mastered the ability to deceive on every level.

The idea that there are many paths to God sounds good and appears to make perfect sense since there are different religions throughout the world. Some of these religions are older than Christianity. Religion is as old as time. There is, however, a great difference between *religion* and a *relationship* to God, and it is only gained through His son, the Lord Jesus Christ.

The Fractured Teachings

The electronic ministry has more than its share of "prosperity" preaching that in the long run is more destructive because it gives a narrow-minded definition of success.

A number of years ago, I was invited to a church by a man I had met during college.

"We have prophetic night on Wednesday nights. Do you prophecy? In our services, everybody gives prophecies, and I'm sure you'll receive one too."

"Is that all you do?" I asked.

"Yes! That's our ministry."

Let me say that personally, I believe in prophecy, and I have both prophesied and received it in my life. But I question a ministry that has become a novelty where everyone is running into one another prophesying. This type of haphazard manner makes one open to demonic spirits and false prophesy, especially if the people have no prayer life or understanding of the Bible. We have the prophetic, and everybody wants a "Word." Often, *the prophetic* cannot be verified by the biblical Word.

I have always questioned the validity of these "prophets" because I'm convinced if the Lord was really doing all of this "speaking," everyone would not be getting a "good" word. This is not to say that Lord does not perform these things; quite the contrary. He does send a prophetic word. But if we only pick out one thing and ignore the rest, it is like a child who only eats sweet things but does not get proper nutrition from greens, broccoli, and peas. We have spiritual malnutrition. Most of these "prophets" do not minister to the spiritual man and, therefore, leave that portion of the man lacking and in great need. While we are trying to get rich and prosper, we are depressed, angry, cannot keep marriages together, and yet the *prophets* keep telling us good things in spite of the fact that many people's lives are falling apart.

The prophets in the Bible days were feared by the people and were not always popular among them because they often brought words of doom and judgment to the people.

Down through the years, I have also had similar invitations to healing nights, blessing nights, anointing nights. Again I have no problem with such things, except when it becomes the entire ministry, and everything else is neglected. There are those that have taken one portion out of the Bible and have built an entire ministry on that one thing while ignoring all the rest.

Silver-Tongued Orators

There are many false doctrines that have been taught down through the millenniums. But as we have moved into the twenty-first-century, revival of some of the older cults along with many new ones have surfaced and taken mainstream, deceiving many. The Bible described these movements and their leaders as *"having a form of godliness, but denying the power thereof"* (2 Tim. 3:5).

Many of these leaders and doctrines have diverted from mainstream teachings and doctrines, many not professing to be Christian at all, and yet it appears that it is becoming more prevalent that Christians are acknowledging and quoting from its leaders and doctrines in mainstream churches. Apostle Paul warned us of "perverted gospels" (Gal. 1:6).

I was listening to a group of Christian ministers as they talked about a popular Muslim minister who spoke at a Christian church. Afterward, the people talked about how good his "sermon" was and how he boldly spoke truth, and they would gladly hear him again.

"He spoke truth that our ministers never say!" one person said to me. (Which upon examination of the sermon, I personally found not to be true.)

Yet in this man's sermon, he never professed what he believed about Christ or what he truly believed religious-wise.

In fact, there was a bold statement affirming that he was a Muslim addressing a Christian church. Which means that this particular church had compromised its faith in Jesus Christ to hear another religious persuasion that does not believe that Jesus is the Christ but merely a prophet, and that the teachings of whom Christianity believes is a false prophet, Mohammed, is who he follows.

So the whole situation is a matter of believers in the true and living God listening to a minister of a false prophet (I will deal with this in greater detail in chapter 12).

Two things I think should be understood. First, the Bible says, *"For the gifts and callings of God are without repentance"* (Rom. 11:29). Meaning a person can be gifted and yet not be saved. People are born with gifts as evident by different skills and abilities that people have since their early days. Therefore, the gift of oration is in many that have not become Christian, but can hold an audience with their gift and abilities.

A survey was recently done concerning the top orators and speeches of history, and among the top was Adolf Hitler, an anti-Semite, a world-leading promoter of genocide and World War II aggressor. Yet the nation of Germany was captivated by his speeches.

The Bible spoke of an occasion when Herod addressed the people with such a profound oration that the people said, *"It is the voice of a god and not the voice of a man"* (Acts 12:21-23).

Unfortunately for this poor fellow, because he did not give God the glory, he was stricken by an angel and was eaten up by worms.

Elijah, the prophet of God, challenged Israel, who had fallen into similar compromise over which god to follow.

> *How long halt ye between two opinions? If the Lord be God, follow him: but if Baal, then follow him. And the people answered him not a word. (1 Kings 18:21)*

Israel had fallen under the same compromising influence that the twenty-first-century church has today. By acknowledging other gods and religious persuasions, we have compromised our faith in the true and living God!

Elijah remained uncompromising in his faith toward the true and living God. His God proved Himself by answering by fire before the nation. This showdown was not settled by speeches but by demonstration. The Bible says,

> *These signs shall follow them that believe: In my name shall they cast out devils; they shall speak with new tongues. They shall take up serpents, and if they drink any deadly thing it shall not hurt them; they shall lay hands on the sick and they shall recover. (Mark 16:17-18)*

King Solomon, the wisest king ever, allowed his many wives and concubines to turn his heart from God.

> *But Solomon loved many strange women…Of the nations concerning which the LORD said unto the children of Israel, Ye shall not go in to them, neither shall they come unto you: for surely they will turn away your heart after their gods: Solomon clave unto these in love. (1 Kings 11:1-2)*

> *And the LORD was angry with Solomon because his heart was turned from the LORD God of Israel, which had appeared unto him twice. (1 Kings 11:9)*

Just like Solomon's heart was turned because of the strange woman who worshipped false gods, the same danger of such compromise with other faiths can happen when we follow after false teachers because of their orations. But signs of demonstration will follow the Spirit-filled uncompromising church.

Chapter Eight

The Megachurch

I have often said Acts 1:8 was not fulfilled until Acts 8:1. By today's definition, the first church would have been considered a megachurch.

On the day of Pentecost after the ascension of the Holy Spirit, the Bible says that after Peter's preaching, three thousand souls were baptized. The church started with three thousand members, and it was growing daily: *"the Lord added to the church daily"* (Acts 2:47). This church was also wealthy.

> *For as many as were possessors of lands or houses sold them, and brought the prices of the things that were sold, And laid them down at the Apostles feet. (Acts 4:34-35)*

There were also a number of miracles that took place, from healing (Acts 3:1-9), to raising the dead (Acts 9:39-41), and miracles of judgment (Acts 5:1-11). Some were released from prison by angels (Acts 5:12-17), all of which validated the church and its purpose. This meant that the early church was a growing wealthy utopia centered in Jerusalem, but they had failed to spread abroad to the world. Instead they stayed in one place. Notice the command from Jesus:

> *Go ye therefore, and teach <u>all nations</u> [my underline] baptizing them in the name of the Father, and the Son, and the Holy Ghost. Teaching them to observe all things whatsoever I have commanded you. (Matt. 28:19-20)*

> *Go ye into all the world, and preach the gospel unto every creature. He that believeth and is baptized shall be saved, but he that believeth not shall be damned. (Mark 16:15-16)*

> *But ye shall receive power, after that the Holy Ghost is come upon you, and ye shall be witnesses unto me in both Jerusalem, and all Judaea, and in Samaria, and unto the uttermost part of the earth. (Acts 1:8)*

Although the Lord's command is clear—to take the gospel message to the world—the early church had limited its ministry to Jerusalem

In comparison to the twenty-first-century megachurch, it is a social club, a fashion show, a "singles' ministry in hopes of meeting a spouse" club, and many other tabs that have been called *ministries* with the wealth of the early church, and yet everyone feels comfortable within the church, but do not carry the gospel message abroad as much as the prosperity, motivational speech, self-worth message. As previously stated, many megachurches are more led by motivational speakers than Bible preachers.

I sometimes hear the "strategies" to get people to come to church. Often these strategies will bring things from the world into the church to encourage people to come in. The problem with this is that what usually brings them in must be maintained to keep them in because their coming in was for the wrong motive in the first place.

However, when one goes out representing the church, there is no need to compromise because by going into an area, one becomes the ambassador of whom they represent. Those who will come in already should know what the church stands for by the representatives it sends out.

The Persecution against the Church

Acts 8:1 talks of the persecution that came against the church and caused it to scatter abroad, which did more to spread the gospel than the megachurch that had become idle in Jerusalem. They ran and scattered so fast until they probably didn't know what direction they were heading when they fled. This is evident because Philip, one of the first deacons of the church whom the Bible described as being full of miracles, and the Holy Ghost would go up to Samaria, a place where the Jews, for racial reasons, were reluctant to go.

When Phillip preached Christ in Samaria, the whole city, because of the gospel message that he preached, lost focus on the fact that he was a Jew but gave heed to his message and received Christ.

> *And the people with one accord gave heed unto those things which Phillip spake, hearing and seeing miracles which he did. For unclean spirits, crying with a loud voice, came out of many that were possessed with them, and many taken with palsies, and were lame, were healed. And there was great joy in the city.* (Acts 8:6-8)

This great revival in Samaria may never have taken place had not God allowed persecution to come against this mega-church at Jerusalem. What Satan meant for evil, God meant for good.

Often, what is lost in this episode is the message of Phillip: he preached Christ. He was uncompromising in his message and pointed them to the cross, the only hope of mankind.

Some modern mega-churches, in order to keep the crowd, may compromise the message, never speaking on or challenging the people, but only delivering "safe sermons," not wanting to offend anyone with a stern warning or challenging sermon. Even Jesus lost all but twelve of the multitudes that followed Him because they were offended by a sermon that he preached (John 6:66-71).

Unfortunately, the larger the church, the more likely scandals will break out, which often can be an embarrassment to the ministry. Sometimes it is because of the lack of right preaching and teaching; other times it is simply percentages (i.e., the more people, the more variance of personalities bound to clash and devils to deal with).

Chapter Nine

We're Dealing with This Kind

I have often said that previous generation of Christians were *"devil-conscious"* to the point where they probably gave Satan more credit than he deserved, attributing everything to him, from failure of mechanical devices like refrigerators or cars to children and spouses. I remember as a youth watching *exorcisms* in church as demons were cast out of individuals by the pastors and elders of the church, sometimes manifesting themselves and even speaking through the victims before being expelled.

One of the problems of the twenty-first-century church is the ignorance of the spirit world. Just as I would see demons cast out and people being delivered a generation ago, I hardly ever see it today. However, just because it is not seen as often as generations past does not mean that demonic powers no longer exist, but that the church has become preoccupied with things like the *prosperity gospel* and can no longer discern spirit activity.

In fact, demonic activity and demonstration of it has increased in recent decades, even finding its place in churches, but unfortunately is not recognized. Jesus, when addressing the seven churches in the book of Revelations, confronted the church of Thyatira:

> *I have a few things against thee, because thou sufferest that woman Jezebel, which calleth herself a prophetess, to teach and to seduce my servants to commit fornication. (Rev. 2:20)*

Similar to the Thyatrian church, the twenty-first-century church has allowed the spirit of Jezebel, among others, to infiltrate that churches and even take high seats and teach false doctrines. Among them are the following:

1) **Witchcraft**—the manipulation or mind control of the congregation through guilt, threats, casting spells, sorcery, and the practice of mysticism.
2) **Disregard or disrespect for authority**—Often a problem in the twenty-first century as a whole but, when in the church, often creates chaos and allows people to act out of a sense of their own rules regardless of established order. When Miriam and Aaron confronted Moses, God smote Miriam with *leprosy (Num 12:10)*.
3) **Rebellion**—*"For rebellion is as the sin of witchcraft, and stubbornness is as the iniquity and idolatry. Because thou hast rejected the word of the LORD"* (1 Sam. 15:23).

I have seen many things brought into the church that shouldn't be, particularly when it comes to certain music and dance because it is birthed out of rebellion or sexual prowess. It is no wonder that the church experiences rebellion and sexual promiscuity, and homosexuality becomes active among the members because of the spirit of Jezebel that we have invited into the church. Often, the argument is made that we need to update, modernize, or brings things into the church that would attract the younger generation. This, however, often brings a compromise and opens the door for other spirits to come into the worship.

In reality, it hasn't won the younger generation except that they're bringing the spirit of the world into the church, causing the purpose of the church to shift the motive, becoming popular with a large congregation, wealthy, but without conviction, deliverance, and often preaching a compromising gospel.

Jesus Warning about Demons

When Jesus sent His disciples on their first mission, they returned rejoicing because *"even the devils are subject to us through thy name" (Luke 10:17).*

Jesus warned them, *"Notwithstanding in this rejoice not. that the spirits are subject to you; but rather rejoice, because your names are written in heaven" (Luke 10:20).*

All spirits are not the same. Just as there are different ranks of angels, so also are there different ranks of demons. Evidently, when Jesus sent His disciples on this mission, they did not encounter high-ranking demons. He, knowing this, cautioned them about rejoicing over how easy it appeared to be to cast them out.

On another occasion, the disciples couldn't cast a demon out of a young boy who suffered with epileptic seizures (Mark 9:14-29). After Jesus cast the demon out of this boy, His disciples were embarrassed by the entire episode and took Him apart privately and asked Him,

> *"Why could we not cast him out?" And He said unto them, "<u>This kind</u> [my underline] can come forth by nothing but by prayer and fasting." (Mark 9:28-29)*

If Jesus said *this kind,* evidently, there are more than one kind. In Luke 10:17, they were dealing with a different kind than in Mark 9. However, the latter was stronger and more resilient than the former. This kind was a higher rank and therefore must be dealt with in a different manner.

Spiritual Rank

I use the term *rank* in remembrance of my military days. When one had higher rank, it meant they had higher authority. To be outranked meant that you were subject to the higher-ranking person. This is not only how the military operates, but in the spirit world as well.

When Jesus said that some demons can only be cast out by prayer and fasting, He was telling us of the rank of various spirits. When the disciples came back rejoicing because the spirits were subject to them, I believe Jesus cautioned them because He knew they had not encountered high-ranking spirits. When they attempted to use the same procedure to cast the demon out of this epileptic boy, *this kind* didn't respond because it outranked the disciples.

When the prophet Daniel sought the Lord with fasting, the angel appeared to him on the twenty-first day:

> *And he said unto me, O Daniel, a man greatly beloved, understand my words that I speak unto thee…*
>
> *from the first day that thou did set thy heart to understand, and chasten thyself before thy God, thy words were heard, and I am come for thy words.*
>
> *But the prince of Persia withstood me one and twenty days, but, lo, Michael, one of the chief princes, came to help me. (Dan. 10:11-13)*

Persia is the ancient name for the modern country of Iran. When the angel spoke of the "Prince of Persia," he was not speaking about a natural prince. A mortal man could not halt an angel. It was the demons, referred to as princes, that sat over and influenced the nation of Persia—politically, socially, religiously, and spiritually. The same is true today as spirits sit over nations, cities, communities, and even homes. This demon was stronger than this angel and withstood him for twenty-one days. The angel had to go back and get help from a stronger angel or higher-ranking angel, also referred to as a prince, to help him get through.

Apostle Paul warned us:

> *For we wrestle not against flesh and blood, but against principalities, against powers, against the rulers of darkness of this world, against spiritual wickedness in high places. (Eph. 6:12)*

Unfortunately, the twenty-first-century church is not willing to do *spiritual warfare* and combat the forces of darkness. And because we have not given ourselves to prayer and fasting, we have no rank to confront demonic spirits, but fear them.

No Prayer Life

I was taught growing up in church that a Christian can be no stronger that his prayer life. Jesus told us, *"Man ought to always pray"* (Luke 18:1). Even though he was the Son of God, He often would pray to His father, sometimes all night.

Prayer is communication with God. With it, we learn and know His will for our lives, become familiar with his voice when His Spirit speaks to our conscience, can be assured and comforted by Him, can be led by Him (Rom. 8:14). Lack of prayer is a lack of communication with the

Lord, and hence, all of the abovementioned are not active in the life of the believer.

When I served in the Marine Corps, I was a communications specialist. It was my job to relay information to ground and air troops from the command center where I was stationed (I was never in combat, but the war games were a part of our training). The importance of my job was such that if the communications broke down, entire missions could fail. Therefore, one of the most important things to me and to those I was communicating with was to make sure that there was always a fresh supply of batteries to keep the lines open and active.

The Holy Spirit is like the batteries in that He keeps the spiritual line open and alive and why it becomes necessary to learn to pray *in the Spirit.*

Knowing the Master's Will

The servant knows the master's will by means of communication. He has a relationship. This is what prayer is to the Christian, communication with the master. A Christian who has no prayer life most likely will walk in error or negligence, not knowing his master's will.

The Bible says, *"For letter killeth, but the Spirit giveth alive"* (2 Cor. 3:6). The Holy Spirit is given to believers who ask for Him. He makes the master's will come alive. Further, it is through Him that the Bible, the infallible word of God, also comes alive. Knowing the will of the master requires that we first get in His will through His written word, the Bible. When we read the word through the guidance and inspiration of the Holy Spirit, drive, desire, and purpose start to intertwine with our spirit. Our spirit is humbled in His presence. So it is when we walk in the presence of God. His presence gives us a confidence. It is gained through prayer and fellowship with Him.

I recall as a boy when I was stalked by a bully on the school playground. He was bigger than me, and I was afraid of him. One day this bully followed me off the school grounds and toward my house. But he made a mistake. He let me get all the way home before he decided to jump on me. At the same time, I saw my father's blue Chevrolet coming around the corner. Being in familiar territory (my house) and my father's presence gave me a confidence that I would not have had on the school playground, and therefore, I was able to beat up the bully, my father eventually having to pull me off him.

Just like my father's presence gave me a confidence to fight and defeat a boy bigger than me, so does the presence of God when we walk close to Him. We walk in fear because we have no confidence or assurance of God's presence.

For God hath not given us the spirit of fear; but of power, and of love, and of a sound mind. (2 Tim. 1:7)

The Fasting Prayer

Prayer and fasting elevate the spiritual rank of the individual. In Saint Matthew's recording, Jesus tells His disciples it was their *unbelief* that handicapped them from casting the demon out (Matt. 17:20). Without a consistent prayer life, there is no fellowship. Without the fellowship, there can be no confidence; and without confidence, there can be no faith.

Fasting is a faith action when one is seeking God out of an urgent motive. By denying oneself of food for a prolonged period, it breaks down humanity and, when accompanied with prayer and consecration, builds up spirituality.

I have done a couple of short fasts lasting anywhere from twenty-four hours to three days. But once I did a fast that lasted ten days. I noticed something different about what I like to refer to as the *journey* of that fast. After three days, the hunger and weakness began to leave, and I found myself into the fourth and fifth day feeling strong and normal. But my senses also became heightened in that smell and hearing became keener. I also found my mind was clearer than usual, and because I did not feel like talking, I didn't do a lot of socializing unless it was necessary. As the days began to progress, I found it easier to pray *in the spirit,* even when I would sit for long meditations in the word.

Even thought it was only ten days, I've known others to go longer, even going as long as twenty-one, thirty, and one man whom I knew went forty days. It is important that when one goes on a prolonged fast that they do as less socializing as possible and spend time in prayer and consecration. As the humanity begins to break down, one also becomes open to ministering spirits that are not always godly. I've known people to go on long fasts, not properly consecrate themselves, and pick up demonic spirits of oppression and confusion.

Fasting heightens one's spirituality and, when done properly, brings to one spiritual power that demons recognize. Fasting and praying bring the believer to a higher spiritual rank, a greater sense of God's presence and power, and its experience increases faith.

Chapter Ten

To Hell with 'Em

I've noticed that the western mind has a tendency to incorporate culture within the worship. There is a reason that Sunday morning in America, it is said, is the most segregated time of the week because blacks worship in a "Black Church," whites worship in a "White Church," Latinos in the "Latino Church," etc. However, I don't think it's necessary because of racism and prejudice as much as it is the variance of culture. Whereas the Black church is more emotional in its worship, whites tend to be more laid-back and subtle. This variance is not only within the worship, but in the culture at large, expressed by music, writings, lingo, etc. The conflict, in some cases, is because one group may not consider or find any values in the variances and arrogantly feel that "we do it right, and you do it wrong!"

Effective ministry takes place when the ministers—whether missionaries, evangelists, or street preachers—understand the culture of the ones to whom they are ministering to and not arrogantly force their own culture upon another in the name of religion. The minister must understand the difference between preaching the gospel to convert the heart and not necessarily the environment. If environmental change *is* necessary, it will only take place with a change of heart, attitude, and mind. The preaching of the gospel does this.

This is one of the reasons why even to this day, the Native Americans still have trouble with American culture because of the way it was *forced* upon them.

The tactics of the American missionaries, when preaching to the Native Americans' general, was done out of disrespect and arrogance as it was already in the minds of these missionaries that the Indian tribes were filled with paganism combined with what they considered stupidity. The accounts of many of the missionaries who ministered to various tribes described them as "savages."

In the 1870s, missionaries sent to share the gospel with the Nez Perce Indians found no success after ten years of preaching and living among them, not winning one convert. One missionary declared that they were all stupid. However, what is obvious is that if you live among a people for ten years and cannot persuade one to accept the good news of the gospel, it is certainly not the fault of the people but the presenter.

The arrogance of many of the missionaries was the idea of converting people into their *own* culture and having no respect or regard for culture of the people they are ministering to. In the case of these missionaries, their mission was not to win the Nez Perce to Christ as much as making them accept white culture and forsake their own, which had great ancestral values and traditions that the white man didn't understand.

The **American Indian boarding schools** established in the latter nineteenth and early twentieth century were for the purpose of educating Native American children according to Euro-American standards. The students were made to dress by the same standards, cut their hair, forsake the traditional "savage" language, learn to speak English, and change their names to traditional "Eurocentric" names. The purpose of this was to *civilize* and *Christianize* the wayward *savages* so that they could be assimilated into the American society.

Some that go in to minister do so in the same manner as the missionaries that went to minister to Native Americans—with a sense of arrogance, feeling everything about them is hopeless, not understanding their culture, and calling them stupid. Just like the missionaries were not effective among the Nez Perce, so it appears many are not effective in the *hood*.

However, the arrogance of racism will always view an "outsider" or an "other" as inferior, no matter how much education or assimilation tactics have been invested into a people, tribe, or nation. Such has been the attitude of the American Christian nation to its own people.

People want to relate to the person who is ministering to them. They are more likely to open up and trust someone whom they feel has been where they are. This is why people whom the Lord has delivered from a particular environment go right back to it to minister (i.e., ex-prisoners ministering in the prisons).

What should also be understood is that everyone does not have a ministry for every type of people. Ministries are effective when its participants *understand* those who they are ministering to. For example, if one has never been in jail or imprisoned, they may not necessarily understand the mind-set of inmates trying to survive in the hostile environment of prison.

I am reminded of the young man I knew who took it upon himself to explain to a group of women how to have a baby. He may have watched his wife give birth, but could not speak other than what he observed. Needless to say, those women, who were highly offended at his advice, got through verbally chewing him up and spitting him out.

One of the attributes of Jesus's ministry was His compassion for people. One of the reasons for His working miracles or crying at the tomb of Lazarus (John 11:35) or His weeping over Jerusalem (Luke 19:41-44) was because he was moved with compassion towards the people. He also saw the potential in people, which is why He never gave up on anybody despite their flaws or fired any of His disciples, including Peter, who denied Him, and Judas, who betrayed Him.

Giving up on a person or desiring that they go to hell is not a good attribute for Christian character. Jesus encountered liars, adulterers, cheaters, and various other types of sinners, even to the criticism of the religious leaders who would have nothing to do with them. Even on the cross,

He asked His father to forgive them *"for they know not what they do"* (Luke 23:34) and forgave the thief that was crucified with Him when he asked for mercy (Luke 23:43).

When Jesus called Matthew (Matt. 9:9), he called him from a job that was despised by the Jews. He was a tax collector for the oppressive Roman government and was considered a sellout by the people. Most tax collectors were dishonest, and Matthew hung out with dishonest friends. But he was so elated that Jesus called him until he made a supper for Jesus and invited all of his friends (Matt. 9:10-13). The whole gang was there, the house was filled with all of Matthew's friends, all of them known for their dishonest reputations, and there sat Jesus in the middle of them. The religious leaders had a problem with it. They asked His disciples, *"Why eateth your master with publicans and sinners?"*

The modern-day comparison would have been equivalent to Jesus sitting and eating with gang members, possibly even drug dealers. Not only did the religious leaders of that day have a problem with it, some of the modern-day ministers would have a problem with it. Yet the response from Jesus is still the same: *"They that are whole need not a physician, but they that are sick"* (v.12).

Jesus's ministry took Him to the people and not just within the religious community. Unlike many of the prayers of church members asking the Lord to "send them in" to our revival, fashion show, or musical, He went out into the streets, marketplace, and gatherings where the people were. In every case, Jesus never went among what many considered undesirables with a condemning message, but a message of hope and to show them that they were just as important to Him as any other person. The same message should be ministered in the *hood*. Many of them have already been deemed worthless by the media, the middle and upper class, and even some of the churches. It was because of hell that Jesus went abroad, preaching the message of hope and eventually going to the cross. Notice how Jesus addresses His cross experience:

> *Greater love no man than this, that man lay down his life for his friends. Ye are my friends, if ye do whatsoever I command you. (John 15:13)*

Because of His compassion, He says,

> *Come unto me, all ye that labour and are heavy laden, and I will give you rest. (Matthew 11:28)*

And therefore, the ministry of Jesus should be the example of the ministry of the church. Christians should not desire or rejoice when they feel that people have gone to hell. If Jesus made the ultimate sacrifice and paid the ultimate price to prevent all from going, we as His followers should take the same attitude and urgency in praying for and witnessing to as many as we come in contact with, even if we are rejected, ridiculed, or abused.

Chapter Eleven

The Twenty-First-Century Church and President Barack Obama

Personally I like President Barack Obama. I first remember him as a skinny candidate for the Illinois Senate, making a speech at our local church. I even shook his hand.

When he became a candidate for the highest office in the land and hence becoming the most powerful man in the world, I was excited and backed his campaign all the way to victory. As an African-American man in America, I was proud, thankful, and have prayed for him every day. That being said, I realize that the man is not a god and is fallible.

President Obama has faced far more challenges as the first Black president than any other who has held the office, as proven by the constant attacks from political enemies and his portrayal as everything from Hitler to the Joker and even Satan.

What I found even more disturbing was the prejudice and racism that came from the white church leaders as during his reelection, they backed a man who was part of a known and denounced cult by evangelicals who suddenly found good Christian values in it and declared it mainstream.

Other Christian leaders prophesied America's downfall because of his election, when it was the previous administration that plunged America into two wars and nearly destroyed the economy.

I would listen to the rhetoric of the *Tea Party* as they said the same things that were said by the Confederate states just before the Civil War: "We need to take our country back!" and "Down with tyranny!", saying and portraying unfaltering images of Obama just like they did Lincoln, even burning him in effigy.

President Obama's agenda to move the country forward was constantly thwarted and attacked by his political enemies for obvious political and racial reasons, having shown their disrespect and disdain for him, yelling out things like "You lie!" at the State of the Union Address, obviously placing these reasons ahead of the best interest of the country, making it difficult, if not impossible, for the president to lead. Still, in spite of this, he accomplished many victories and was reelected when *experts* predicted a landslide defeat.

Obama and the Gay Agenda

President Obama was not the originator of gays' rights from the White House as President Bill Clinton was the originator of rights for gays in the military, compromising with the "Don't ask, don't tell" policy. But Obama pushed more aggressively for the rights of gays and the repealing of "Don't ask, don't tell" where gays could openly, without prejudice, serve in the military.

However, the gay agenda in the Obama administration became a *runaway train* that eventually allowed gays to marry with the backing and blessings of the Obama administration with the president himself speaking in favor of this *abomination.*

President Obama has publicly congratulated many celebrities for "coming out," calling them heroes, hence, insulting those that have placed their lives on the line or even given their lives for the freedoms of this nation.

Although I *do* fault the president for this, I think that there is something that should be considered about the president's attitude toward gays. President Obama, as a Black man in America, is a product of an environment that has been discriminatory toward minorities for centuries. What Black man in America has not felt the shame and pain of racial prejudice or racial profiling? This automatically will make a person who has been victim of such prejudice feel sympathetic toward those of similar fate.

President Obama, being the master politician (no man could have become president unless he was) could feel the climate of the country that was changing since many high-profile homosexuals were coming out of the "closet," even riding on the coattails of the Civil Rights movements of the '60s and comparing themselves to the leaders and martyrs that fought and died for equality.

Gay Rights vs. Civil Rights

In America, people have the right and free will of expression, religion, and the pursuit of happiness. These are basic rights of every citizen. It is against the law to be discriminated against because of race, gender, or religion. It is not necessary to make laws or pass laws that are already guaranteed by the Constitution. Yet the gay rights agenda now wants the right to marry, hence making it a state-sanctioned union. This is in direct clash with many religious views, particularly Christianity.

The problem I have with this is that the Civil Rights movement was a stand against racial discrimination, discrimination because of what a person *could not help* or change (skin color), not what *could be helped* or changed as in behavior. A person does not have to engage in sex; homosexual like heterosexual is an *action* or better described as *behavior*. Heterosexual sins, fornication, and adultery are not civil rights. They are behavioral actions, which are committed without the benefit of governmental recognition or state sanction.

Homosexuals have tried to say that their *behavior* is in them from birth (i.e., "I am born this way"), even going as far as to talk about the possibility of a "gay gene," a theory not backed by fact:

> *Geneticist have gone so far as to purpose the existence of a gay gene that all animals and humans contain within them and which is turned on and off like a switch depending on the circum-stances of the individual. But the gay gene has eluded discovery despite 2 decades of enthusiastic anticipation.*
>
> *The Human Genome Project in which has identified between 20,000 and 25,000 genes without finding evidence of a gay gene.*[2]

Another statistic that is not often discussed is the consequences and effects of the gay lifestyle. Among them is that the suicide rate among gay males is 28%, and that the lifespan among gays is reduced by 20% behind obesity, cigarette smoking, alcoholism, and heroin addiction.[3] To simply put it, being gay is not only sin, it is unhealthy.

The twenty-first century has seen a drastic change of culture that was birthed with the attitudes of the '60s as spelled out by best-selling author Mr. Larry Tomczak:

> *Abortion demands intensified as all the "Make love—not war" mantras spawned unwanted babies. Soon abortion was legalized.*

---

[2] Roger Denson, "Homosexuality as Population Control?", *Huff Post World,* November 2, 2013.

[3] Meredith Roderick, "What Is Wrong with Same-Sex Marriage," *Tomorrow's World Magazine,* July-August 2013, p.6.

Divorce laws were liberalized (today 80% of divorces are "no fault," translating into 45 million divorces since the end of the '60s!) Sexual standards evaporated and resulted in rampant pornography, skyrocketing out-of-wedlock births, one in every four teens strapped with a sexually transmitted disease, drug abuse, school violence, teen suicide, spousal and child abuse, violent crime, prison overpopulation, sexual anarchy, gender confusion, glamorizing and promotion of homosexuality, lesbianism, bisexuality, and trans-genderism with gender reassignment surgeries. All of this proliferating since the now infamous "Summer of Love" soured to a stench.

Dr. James Dobson identified six lies that are now accepted:

Premarital, extramarital and traditionally abnormal sex are moral and healthy. There should be no sanctity of human life in law. Drug use makes great recreational sport.

Divorce offers an easy escape from marriage.

Marriage should be redefined to include same-sex unions. God is dead—at least make it appear that way by systematically airbrushing Him from society.[4]

What even pushed this agenda further was the attitude of the twenty-first-century church that now began to change its views of homosexuality, no longer calling it an abomination, but rather compromising the scriptures for *modern thought.*

Religious leaders that hold fast to the Holy scriptures of the Bible blame Obama, and although he is not without fault, it is a combination of things aforementioned and others not mentioned that have brought America to this state. Obama, as much as he has tried to be president of all people and not just Black people, is still a product of discrimination that America has produced. Therefore, his agenda of uplifting the *downtrodden* has focused on the group discriminated against for their behavior and placing them in the same category as other minorities who have suffered at the hands of American prejudice for centuries.

Further, President Obama was the product of a church that did not speak out against homosexuality and, like many of the churches, have compromised on this stand today. He has the approval of many religious leaders surrounding him.

Most White religious leaders who see the wrong in President Obama's backing and *political promoting* of gay

---

[4.] Larry Tomczak, "6 Lies from the pit of Hell That are Destroying America," *Charismatic News*, July 9, 2015.

marriage fail to take into consideration that it is the product of discrimination, which White America has practiced against Black people for centuries, often in the name of religion, and now it has morphed with multiple arms.

This is not to condone the President's actions, but to point out that his attitudes toward gays is an extension of sympathetic thought because of what most minorities have experienced in America.

Many Black Americans are still the victim of racist culture. Many White Christians who, in most cases, have not been the victim of America's racial discrimination nor racial profiling still find themselves unsympathetic.

The religious world has now also seen a rise of "gay" Christians, those professing to know Christ and yet maintain a gay lifestyle. There is also a rise of openly gay churches; often the minister is gay and living with a same-sex spouse.

In the latest study, about 17% of congregations said they had openly gay and lesbian members. Open gay and lesbian members were more prevalent in larger congregations. Overall, 31% of the congregations members were part of communities with openly gay and lesbian people.

This shows that the attitude of Christianity toward gays in the past twenty-five years has run parallel with the changing American culture as the attitudes in the past twenty-five years have changed to a more favorable acceptance.

Even among American Jews, the support for gay marriage is 81%.[5]

Laws are now being considered in several states that would make it illegal to attempt to *covert* homosexual to heterosexual. The ban would prohibit mental health professionals and social workers from performing therapy that tries to change the sexual orientation of children. In addition, the American Psychological Association highly opposes gay conversion therapy.[6]

The challenge of the twenty-first-century church does not just come from the change of American culture toward homosexuality, but from within Christendom itself as many denominations have compromised or forsaken the teachings of the Bible as many ministers and priests are "coming out," declaring their Christian Faith is in accordance with their lifestyle. This despite the fact that scriptures call this *"Uncleanness, Abomination, Fornication, Strange Flesh"* (Lev. 18:22, Rom. 1:27, 1 Cor. 6:9-10, Jude 1:7).

Because abortion and homosexuality are depleting the American population, most financial experts say in the long run, it will have a negative effect on the American economy as well and in the long run threaten America's status as a superpower.

[5.] Molly Ball, "The Quiet Gay-Rights Revolution in America's Churches," *The Atlantic*, August 14, 2013.

[6.] Marina Fang, "The Country's First Openly Bisexual Governor Bans Gay Conversion Therapy in Her State," *The Huffington Post*, May 19, 2015.

States with same-sex marriage have seen a decline in opposite sex marriage by at least 5%...that unmarried women are more likely to get abortions, and additional 900,000.[7]

[7.] Pema Levy, "The Science of How Gay Marriage Will Destroy America," *Mother* Jones, April 27, 2015.

Chapter Twelve

The Emergence of Islam in America

Islam says it is the fastest-growing religion in the world. Although there may be some truth to this, originally it was not because of conversion, but rather birth rate among Islamic countries. However, because many of the Churches have forsaken the true Gospel and are compromising, embracing what Apostle Paul described as perverted gospel (Gal. 1:6-9), it has become easier for Islam to influence Christianity and even overtaking many European churches as well as influence American churches.

Many churches in America are trying to find "common ground" among the two religions, even going as far as to have "fellowship services," not always realizing that the God of the Bible is not the same as the god of Islam while violating the scripture that says, *"Have no fellowship with the unfruitful works of darkness"* (Eph. 5:11). It is easy to say that God is the same god in all religions, but this is not true.

Islamic Indoctrination in America's Youth

For whatever reason, some of the school systems in America feel the need to introduce Islam. It is not just for social studies or world history, but in some cases, it goes as far as to indoctrinate them with Islamic rules and customs:

> *In its latest report, the American Center for Law and Justice (ACLJ) said students in US public schools are now being forced to learn how to convert to Islam and recite "Allah is the only God."*
>
> *The ACLU said it is now taking action against schools that censor Christianity and promote Islam.*[8]

However, what I find interesting particularly with the emergence of the more radical Islamic groups is that they are not only a menace to the Christian community in Moslem countries, but to the traditional Muslims as well. An interview was done with a Lebanon Christian after the city had been overtaken by one of the radical Muslim groups:

> *Previous to this invasion the Christians and Muslims got along just fine. Now with ISIS coming in they are creating problems for everyone all around.*

[8.] Czarina Ong, "Outrage Against Christians: Public Schools in US shun Christianity, Welcome Islam," *Christianity Today*, September 16, 2015.

The radical Muslims, armed with such words as *Jihad* and *Sharia Law*, are terrorists in every form, often giving their victims both Christian and Muslim a choice of converting to their way of thinking or face death. In the eyes of these groups, America is the "Great Satan," and Israel is the "Little Satan."

America's traditional Christian values and teachings are now being compromised, hence the introduction to alternative religions and less emphasis on Christianity, particularly to the upcoming generation, is slowly but surely turning America away from the God of the Bible. This is one of the challenges of the twenty-first-century church.

Who Is Allah?

Although many people feel that Allah is another word for God and feel comfortable using it interchangeably, its origin is pagan, originally a moon deity. The original Arabic word, translated *Allah,* meaning *"the god,"* was also found in the Kabah in Mecca, a shrine built during pre-Islamic time recognizing 350 different gods. Among them is the Hubal idol on the roof the Kaaba. This idol was one of the chief deities of the ruling Quraysh.

> *The idol was made of red agate and shaped like a human, but with the right hand broken off and replaced with a golden hand. When the idol was*

moved inside the Kaaba, it had seven arrows in front of it, which were used for divination.[9]

Although Christianity is often accused of pagan practice by Islam, Islam also incorporated much of the Arabs' pagan worship in its practice as well. In fact, Allah was the female deity married to the sun god and having three daughters, Allat, Alluzah, and Manat, otherwise known as the daughters of Allah, which were known among Arabs before Islam and of which Muhammad's family was a worshipper. The crescent moon came from this god and is still the symbol for Islam today. Religious rites are also still planned around the lunar calendar, such as the Ramadan fast.

Some scholars have made a comparison between Islam and the ancient worship of Baal, who was worshipped in Babylon, which was located in the modern-day country of Iraq. According to the *Encyclopedia of Religion*, Allah compares with Bel (Baal).[10] It involves the worship of the sun and moon.

---

[9] Francis E. Peters, *Muhammad and the Origins of Islam* (New York: SUNY Press, 1994).

[10] *Encyclopedia of Religion Corpus Publisher* (1979).

Hubel is believed by some scholars to be the ancient god of the Moabites when the pre-Islamic Meccans took over the temple.[11]

In Islam, Allah is not seen as a father but rather a master, and the servant cannot obtain any greater intimacy with him.

Muslim writer Shabbir Akhtar states it this way:

Muslims do not see God as their father or equivalently, themselves as the children of God. Men are servant of a just master: they cannot in Orthodox Islam, typically attain any greater degree of intimacy with their creator.[12]

Therefore, the intimacy and loving relationship is absent in Islam. This is one of the reasons why Muslims don't believe that Jesus is the "Son" of God because if Allah had a son, who is his mother?

This goes back to the erroneous teaching Mohammed received as a youth about the Catholic insistence that Mary is the mother of Christ or "Mother of God."

Akhtbar again states,

[11.] Dunkin, Timothy, Baal, Hubal, and Allah. "A Rebuttal to the Islamic Article entitled 'Is Hubel and Allah the Same?' by MD SM Saifullah and David Abdullah."

[12.] Shabbir Akhtbar, *A Faith for All Seasons* (Chicago: Ivan R Dee Publisher, 1990), p.129.

The Koran, unlike the Gospel, never comments of the essence of Allah. "Allah is wise" or "Allah is loving" may be pieces of revealed information, but in contrast to Christianity, Muslims are not enticed to claim that "Allah is love" or "Allah is wisdom" Only adjectival descriptions are attributed to the divine being and these merely as they bear revelation of God's will for man. The rest remains mysterious.[13]

Al-Ghazali, a prominent theologian and Muslim scholar, says,

The end result of the Arifin[14] *is the inability to know him, and their knowledge is, in truth, that they do not know him, and that it is impossible for them to know him.*[15]

The Spread of Islam

When Muhammad went to Medina after being exiled from Mecca, he initially allied himself with the Arab Jews, even seeing himself as a reformer of Judaism, encouraging everyone to pray toward the Holy City of Jerusalem.

[13.] Ibid.
[14.] Arifin—the religion of Islam, based upon the teachings of Muhammad. *The Knowers,* used by the mystics in the sense of gnostics
[15.] Fadlou Shehadi, *Ghazali's Unique Unknowable God* (Leiden, E.J. Brill 1964), p.34.

But the Jews rejected him as a prophet, mainly because he did not know the Torah (except for certain excerpts he picked up, possibly from a companion), and he grew hostile toward them.

He later allied himself with the Sebeans, who also practice the religion of the moon deities. Muhammad declared himself a prophet of Allah and was accepted. Because of this, he was able to raise a military and go back to Mecca, conquering the city, making war and conquering many cities in his route back.

After the death of Muhammad in AD 632, the radical spread of this religion began to go into much of the Middle Eastern Mediterranean regions and Africa in what is historically known as the *Arab Conquest of the Seventh Century*. The conquering of these nations was done in the name of the Islamic religion. Historically, nations were not *converted*, but *conquered* into Islam by warfare and bloodshed.

Further, the Koran is not in unison with the Bible and is contradictory. Muslims believe that it was Ishmael whom Abraham was about to sacrifice on the altar instead of Isaac, as the Bible says. In Islam, Jesus was not the Christ, the Son of God, but was a prophet. The Koran teaches that man is morally good while the Bible says there is none righteous. The Koran teaches that man can gain Paradise by good works; the Bible teaches that salvation is only in the redemptive work of Christ and that by accepting Him as Lord and Savior is the only way to God.

Jesus said, *"Go into all the world and preach the gospel"* as the means for converting souls into the kingdom. Islam desires to convert the world to the Islamic system through Jihad (Holy War).

The Nation of Islam

The Nation of Islam is the highest-profile Muslim group in America, also called Black Muslims, and although this group is not recognized as true Muslims among orthodox Muslims (which is not uncommon because various Muslim groups around the world consider many other Muslim groups infidels), it probably has the highest profile among Muslim groups in America.

Minister Louis Farrakhan's greatest triumph as a leader was orchestrating the Million Man March in Washington, DC, on October 16, 1995, with some researchers estimating the crowd as high as 837,000, making it one of the largest gatherings on the Washington Mall. It addressed such issues as racial equality, Black unemployment, making atonement, and Black unity, with various speakers from the Black community. It was a great triumph for Minister Farrakhan.

However, it should be understood that the purpose of the march was not to convert the attendees to Islam. Nationwide, it secured Minister Farrakhan as a national leader, but worldwide, it gave him and the Nation of Islam (NOI) credibility in the Muslim world.

I've noticed that Minister Farrakhan has been invited to many Christian churches, often stirring the congregations like a revival evangelist and leaving many of them to wonder if there is really a difference between what he preaches and what Christian ministers *ought* to be preaching.

However, there is something that should be understood about this charismatic orator and what he really believes.

The founder of the NOI was a man by the name of Wallace D. Farad or Wallace Farad Muhammad. He was succeeded in 1934 by Elijah Muhammed, originally Elijah Poole, born in Sandersville, Georgia, the son of a Baptist minister. Being raised in the South, he was all too familiar with racism and discrimination against Black people.

Poole was a protégé of Farad, who told him that the Black man was a part of the lost tribe of Shabazz, exiled in America.

What is further interesting to note about the foundational teachings of the NOI are the words of Elijah Muhammad himself, who states in his book about Farad, *Message to the Black Man,*

> I asked him [Farad], "Who are you, and what is your real name?" He said, "I am the one that the world has been expecting for the past 2000 years." I said to Him again, "What is your name?" He said, My name is Mahdi [Messiah]; I am God.[16]

There are a number of discrepancies as to exactly who Farad was. First, in known pictures of Farad, he appears to

---

[16.] Elijah Muhammed, *Message to the Blackman in America* (Chicago: Muhammad's Temple No. 2, 1965).

be a white man. Second, there appears to be criminal records of Farad on file, and he spent time in San Quentin Prison for, among other things, selling narcotics. Mug shots have appeared with a number of aliases: Wallace Ford, Wallace Dodd, Wali Muhammad.

Historians have used public records to identify Farad as Wallace Dodd Ford. a leader in the Moorish Science Temple. A 1920 census reported his race as white living in Los Angeles, and his father was British.

A news article that appeared in the *Los Angeles Herald Examiner* on July 28, 1963, by Ed Montgomery states,

> *Black Muslims by the thousands pay homage to Wallace Farad founder of the black supremacy cult as one of their own... Yet Wallace Farad is, admittedly, an enterprising, racketeering fake. He is not a Negro. He is a white man.*
>
> *His true name is Wallace Dodd. He was born in New Zeeland on February 26, 1891. His father was British, arriving in New Zeeland via Australia on a sailing Schooner. His mother was a Polynesian native.*[17]

This created an interesting twist to the doctrine of NOI as preached by Elijah Muhammad, who preached

---

[17.] Ed Montgomery, *Los Angeles Herald Examiner*, July 28, 1963.

that the White race was a created race by Yacub the mad scientist.[18] This would mean that if the white race was a race of *created devils* and that Farad was a white man, then his mentor was a devil.

Minister Louis Farrakhan, whenever he addresses a gathering, usually states,

God who came in the form a Master WD Farad.

Thus, also declaring what Elijah Muhammad says, that Farad is God. Certainly the Christian should not be following nor inviting a man into the church to address the congregation when that person is declaring a different *god* than the God of the Bible, no matter how good of an orator or preacher he may be.

This same type of deception has been used by Satan to do the following:

1) Convince a portion of the angelic beings to rebel against God (2 Pet. 2:4).
2) Convince mankind in the Garden of Eden to disobey God. The consequence being exiled from Paradise (Gen. 3:1-24).
3) Convince one of Jesus's own disciples to betray Him.

[18.] Muhammad, "The Making of the Devil."

Apostle Paul warned us:

I marvel that ye are so soon removed from him that is called you into the grace of Christ unto another gospel.

Which is not another; but there be some that trouble you, and would pervert the gospel of Christ.

But though we or an angel from heaven, preach any other gospel unto you than that which we have preached unto you, let him be accursed.

As we said before, so say I again, If any man preach any other gospel unto you than that ye have received, let him be accursed. (Gal. 6:6-9)

The Falsehood of Chrislam

Another false teaching that has recently come to light is *Chrislam:* the merging of Christianity and Islam, despite the fact that the concept of God and Allah are not the same and the Bible and Koran are not compatible.

Clearly, Islam and Christianity are mutually exclusive. Both claim to be the only true way to God, both cannot be right. There is no atonement in Islam, no forgiveness, no savior, and no assurance of eternal life. The Gospel of Jesus Christ is a message of hope; Islam is a religion of hopelessness. (Dr. John F. MacAthur)[19]

Therefore, it would seem obvious that the contradictions between the two religions outweigh the possible unity in merging. For example, When Jesus said, *"I am the way, the truth and the life: no man cometh to the Father, but by me"* (John 14:6), true Bible-believing Christians reject the idea of Muhammad being placed on the same level as Jesus or as an alternative to salvation.

When Chrislam was introduced to Westminster Abbey/the Church of England, Archbishop Cranner responded,

Jesus as a prophet is common to Christianity and Islam and Mohammed is a prophet of Islam alone.

Cranner continues: "Mustafa is an epithet ascribed by Muslims to Mohammed: it means The Chosen One."

He notes that the Abbey did not offer a translation of this term and says that had it been rendered in English during a Christian service, it "would have caused undoubted offence".

[19.] Dr. James MacArthur is a pastor of Grace Community Church, Los Angeles, California, and author. Article appeared in Beliefnet News.

Rev Dominic Stockford, pastor of Christ Church, Teddington and chairman of the Protestant Truth Society said: "The recent use of a prayer equating Muhammad with Jesus, used in Westminster Abbey, was the latest in a string of shocking steps taken by the Church of England recently. And for it to be read out in Turkish, contrary to Article XXIV, being as it was 'a tongue not understood of the people' compounds the matter."

He continued: "How any Christian can think that Jesus and Muhammad can be put together as prophets is beyond me. For one thing, Jesus is no mere prophet, but is Saviour and Lord. The Bible is clear as can be that there is only one God, and that there is only one way to God—and they are Jesus own words which clarify this: 'Jesus said to him, "I am the way, and the truth, and the life; no one comes to the Father but through Me."' (John 14:6).

And for another, the religion of Islam is contrary to that of Christianity, denying as it does the divinity of Jesus Christ, and even denying that God has a Son (Surah 19:35-36), a Divinity and a Sonship without which Jesus could be no Saviour.[20]

[20.] Prophecy News Watch, May 26, 2015, /html#spZLUUtgV2vtidyu.99.

In fact, Chrislam is best described as those believing in neither Christianity nor Islam, but would more refer to the ancient sect of Nestorism, a sect considered heretic by the Council of Ephesus in the fifth century.

By placing Christ on the same level as Muhammad further shows that the believer in such misunderstands the sin nature of mankind, and hence, the need for a savior. This, therefore, would simply dilute the gospel message and put Chrislam into the category of all religions, trying to find and combine the good in everything and make one religion, which has been the failure of religion throughout the ages. As Archbishop Canner stated, *"Jesus is no mere prophet, but is Savior and Lord."*

And yet some Muslims believe that Muhammad is the perfect man and not Christ.

> *For Muslims, Muhammad and not Isa (Jesus) is the perfect man, the God-given perfect example. Muhammad is seen as vastly superior to Isa, and in Islamic is widespread…He has become an eternal figure, for whose sake God created the world, the only real intercessor and mediator.*[21]

Hence, the religions are not even compatible and therefore cannot be comparable.

[21.] Patrick Sookhdeo, *Is the Muslim the Biblical Jesus?* (Virginia: Isaac Publishing Mclean, 2012), p.18.

Chapter Thirteen

New Age and Pantheism

Now the Spirit speaketh expressingly, that in the latter times some shall depart from the faith, giving heed to seducing spirits, and doctrines of devils.
—*1 Timothy 1:4*

*P*antheism is the belief that God is in everything and everybody and that God *is* everything and everybody. It is found in many religions and particularly in the *New Age Religion.* It has become a part of the main philosophy of *New Age* with devoted followers such as actress Shirley Maclaine and renowned talk show host Oprah Winfrey and is a driving force behind the feminist movement.

Douglas R. Groothuis, research associate with Probe Ministries (Seattle, Washington) identifies six distinct characteristics of New Age thinking:

1) All is one.

2) All is God.
3) Humanity is God.
4) A change in consciousness.
5) All religions are the same.
6) Cosmic evolutionary optimism.

Within *New Age*, God is represented as both masculine and feminine or exclusively feminine by the mythological Gaia or "Mother Earth." Though this idea may be popular among New Agers, the Bible says,

> *Professing themselves to be wise, they became fools and changed the glory of the uncorruptible God into an image. (Rom. 1:22-23)*

> *Who changed the truth of God into a lie, and worshipped and served the creature rather than the Creator, who is blessed forever. Amen. (Rom. 1:25)*

New Age's religious experience is through spirit-counsel, psychotechnology, extraterrestrials and even drug-induced meditations to encounter demons.

Such an idea also believes that there is no sin, and therefore, redemption is not necessary; that God is an impersonal god who only requires that each person do the best that they can, that there are no miracles except the miracle of nature itself, and that life is one with the universe. The popularity of such thought was originated by Benedict De Spinoza when his *Ethics* philosophical treaties was first published in 1677 and has evolved, including portions of Buddhism, Hinduism, and yoga becoming the New Age movement of the '70s.

Pantheism is preached by, among others, Eckhart Tolle, who wrote the book *The Power of Now* on the subject and, in 2009, sold over three million copies and has been translated into thirty-three different languages. One reviewer described it as *"Buddhism mixed with mysticism and a few references to Jesus Christ, a sort of New Age reworking of Zen"* In 2008, the *New York Times* referred to Tolle as "the most popular spiritual author in the United States."

Many Christians have departed from traditional teachings, forsaking the scriptures and are following this ideology because of its appeal, erroneously thinking that it is an expansion or a greater insight to religion, philosophy, and human consciousness, when in reality, it is a spiritual deception leading many down the wrong path. The Bible warned of those

> *Having a form of godliness, but denying the power thereof: from such turn away. (2 Tim. 3:5)*

Tolle, is often a guest of one of his biggest supporter of his theories, Oprah Winfrey, who herself has stated,

> *One of the mistakes that humans beings make is that there is only one way…there could not possibly be one way…There are many ways to God.*

She came to this conclusion when she stated, "I took God out of the box." This is rejecting what has been taught about God, His nature, the sin of man, and the need for a savior. This begins to lead one down another path, a path of deception that Satan is all too pleased to show, especially if one has already rejected the idea that there is only one true path to God.

Pantheism feels that religion is not necessary and that one makes his/her own quest and destiny by living only in the present. Tolle writes in the third chapter of his book, *The Power of Now*:[22]

> *You cannot find yourself going into the past. You cannot find yourself coming into the present. Life is now. There was never a time when your life was not now, nor will there ever be.*

The popularity of such philosophy, however, denies sin, the transgression that takes one out fellowship with God. Jesus said, *"If any man will come after me let him deny himself"* (Matt. 16:24).

Further, it becomes easy for those of the western mind (meaning in America) to deny the past or future when the present is not engulfed in the troubles and tragedies that plague this world, particularly in war-torn and pov-

---

[22.] Eckhart Tolle, *The Power of Now* (1997).

erty-stricken countries and the future where death is all around.

One Pantheist explained that the universe responds to the message that we send to it through our thoughts and attitude. Again, as if making God impersonal and calling the universe, which was the created, the creator.

Despite how logical or how much things appeal to the intellect, one must remember the warning from the Bible:

> *There is a way which seemeth right unto a man, but the end thereof are the ways of death. (Prov. 14:12)*

Satan's tactic from deceiving angels to mankind has been to play on the logic of one's thought. It's all part of deception to divert one from the true path to God through His son Jesus Christ alone.

Chapter Fourteen

The Relevance and Power of the True Gospel Message

The Gospel has not nor will it ever change. It is the Word of God, and He never changes. *"For I am the LORD, I change not"* (Mal. 3:6). The Word is true, and the minister must be fully convinced of this and preach it with conviction.

When Jesus said, *"I am the way, the truth, and the life: no man cometh unto the Father, but by me"* (John 14:6), in the twenty-first century, this statement is both offensive and *politically incorrect.* This emphatically states that all other religions are wrong, hopeless, and vain. It is not a matter of choosing which religion to follow or gaining heaven by doing the best you can.

The gravity of such a statement is offensive to all other religions because it is basically saying that Islam, Buddhism, Hinduism, New Age, Pantheism, and all other religions are *lies*, and therefore, professing Christians who believe that there are other paths to God besides Christ are not walking to true fellowship with Christ.

Unfortunately, there are many high-profile Christian ministers who have bought into the "New Age" philosophy and the fellowship of other religions and are compromising the true gospel of Jesus Christ for political correctness. In all of mankind's existence, there has never been an atheistic culture. (There have been atheistic governments. But even they could not suppress or stop the movement of the gospel throughout their nations.) Religion is as old as time. But even religion alone cannot change the hearts of men. It is designed to change men from the outside and put it inside with rules, philosophies, and teachings. The Word of God, however, has always been relevant because it changes men from the inside out.

Jesus did not come to start another religion. If religion alone could have saved mankind, it never would have been necessary for Jesus to come. It is flawed, has created wars, slavery, self-righteousness, made some feel better than others. The first murder committed (Cain killed his brother Abel) was over a difference of religious practice. It still has the same flaws today as wars are still fought and murders are still committed, rapes still occur, all in the name of religion.

Although the cultures are different, the message is the same. The Gospel is the Good News that Jesus Christ has redeemed mankind from his sin.

Ministering to the Next Generation

It should be understood that the entire group or *race* cannot be defined by one culture as the influences vary from different neighborhoods, religious upbringings, and class status. This type of influence is common among all ethnic groups in America. All Blacks do not think and act the same, no more than the Italian, Irish, Polish, Jews, or any other ethnic groups. Even the cultures among the Native American tribes vary, and yet they are still a part of the American culture. After all, Native Americans preceded all others in this land.

The Civil Rights Movement of the '50s and '60s was less passive than the revolutionaries of the '70s. The beginning of the movement was inspired by Christian principle by member of the church. Its early leaders were ministers. It is the youth that generally change the culture because of its exposure and openness to those that they become exposed to. The Civil Rights Movement began to see a shift when the young revolutionaries used more radical tactics in an attempt to bring change to the society. What is interesting to note about the more radical tactics was that the FBI among others, began to move more aggressively to squelch the movement because the powers that be considered the aggressive approach to be a threat.

The Culture in the Hood

Modern technology has made the world smaller. Because it is smaller it now makes one more easily exposed to other cultures from around the world. Whereas America has been predominately Christian since its inception, modern technology such as the Internet has allowed us to explore and connect to cultures all around the world.

In Mark 16:15, Christ commands us to go into all the world and make disciples. Jesus told Saint Peter, *"I will make you a fisher of men."*

Ministering within the *Hood*, or the community surrounded by drugs, violence, and gangs, is not the same as ministering to the community with less violence. The way of "survival" is often the way of the "hood."

I recall seeing a documentary on TV a number of years ago on the subject of young gang members, some of them as young as eight and ten years old. Most of these had already dropped out of school, were being raised by a single parent, usually the mother, and had seen many of their peers die violently to gang warfare. The saddest thing I remember was an interview with an eight-year-old boy who said he did not expect to live to see adulthood and had seen a number of his young friends killed. While most young boys had ambitions of growing up and one day playing ball or becoming architect or having a role model to pattern themselves after, their desire was to be part of a gang and carry a pistol.

The trophy of these youth was to have an expensive pair of gym shoes worn by a famous athlete, even though the shoes costs more than any of them had. Some were even willing to kill for the shoes and fight if anyone stepped on or scoffed them. Although many of these youth were in their early teens, they had experienced enough of hard life to put them in a much higher age mentality. How do we minister to these young people?

How would Jesus minister to them? Let's go back to His time and see an example. There is a core in every person that, although they live in a different environment, they have basic emotions and needs. The core of man each is nurtured by his surroundings. Jesus's disciple Peter was not in a gang of sorts, but he had a leadership personality as well as a temper. His upbringing and occupation as a fisherman brought out certain traits as well as passions. He seemed certain of himself and was not going to back down to any man. Peter would fight and although much is made of his denial of Jesus, it should be remembered that in the Garden of Gethsemane he *did* fight, cutting off a man's ear (John 18:10).

He would have fit in perfect in the *hood*, possibly even being a gang leader. He had the leadership quality. He had the temper and quite possibly would have been intolerant. He had the business sense to set up what drug dealers refer to as an "enterprise."

The first thing Jesus says to Peter is, *"Follow me and I will make you a fisher of men"* (Matt. 4:19). He relates to what Peter does for a living. He uses what Peter is familiar with to simplify his purpose. If Peter was a twenty-first-century gang leader in the *hood*, He might have said, *"Follow me and instead of destroying men, I will show you how to build them."*

When Jesus performs the miracle of the great catch of fish (Luke 5:1-10), Peter is not only astonished but convicted. He sees the light of Jesus and when comparing it to himself he feels unworthy to stand before the Lord. He confesses of being a sinner. *"Depart from me; for I am a sinful man O Lord"* (v. 8). Jesus does not condemn him or reprimand him for his sinful lifestyle. But He gives him purpose: *"Henceforth thou shalt catch men"* (v. 10).

The Ministry of Jesus

When one looks at the Ministry of Jesus, it is clear that He knew the affective way of ministering to the people was to speak to them where they were. I am reminded of a religious forum I was in a number of years ago. One of the speakers was given the platform and proceeded to speak about forty-five minutes on a subject that I don't remember. The one thing I do remember about his presentation was that it was extremely boring and did not hold my attention longer than three minutes. Afterward, I was in the office with the pastor and a few of the other ministers.

"How was the presentation?" he asked.

"Boring!" was the overwhelming response.

One minister even said, "He spoke too much Greek and Hebrew for me."

The pastor responded by saying something that to this day has often stills stays in my mind. "People who are trying to impress everyone with how much they know usually only impress themselves."

Jesus never tried to impress people with what He knew. After all, He knew everything. He ministered to the people where they were. He told stories that related to their everyday lives. In order to effectively minister to the culture, one must first understand the culture. One must also understand that to talk down to something that you don't understand makes one look arrogant to the ones he is attempting to minister to.

Going back to the words of the pastor who made the statement, "People who are trying to impress everyone with how much they know usually only impress themselves." It is a form of arrogance that places one above the other, at least in his own mind. This is not effective ministry. One forgets the purpose of ministry. Again, let us learn from the example of Jesus. *"The Son of man did not come to be ministered unto, but to minister"* (Matt. 20:28). Although the gospel message is the same, the presentation is what makes the difference. The Bible says, *"...He that winneth souls is wise"* (Prov. 11:30).

The failure of ministry takes place because the messenger may well be aware of what the message is, but does know to whom the message is being presented to. Again, look at the ministry of Jesus. He knew the mind-set of the people, and when He preached, He used parables, simply stories that the common man understood.

Apostle James states,

> *If a brother or sister be naked, and destitute of daily food, And one of you say unto them, "Depart in peace, be ye warmed and filled; notwithstanding ye give them not those things which are needful to the body; what doth it profit?" (James 2:15-16)*

You cannot effectively minister to a hungry man without feeding him first.

When ministering, one must ask oneself the question, Is what I am saying or the tactic I'm using relevant? Of course the Gospel always is, but am I presenting it in a way that the people can relate to? Do I present myself as a humble messenger to the people or as a condemner wrapped in self-righteousness?

I worked for a Christian publishing company that published books and gospel tracts. Among the tracts was one called "Here's a Tip," designed for waitresses in restaurants. Instead of leaving money for the waitress, Christians would leave this gospel tract to share the message of Christ. However, the company soon received a number of letters from waitresses and restaurant owners asking them to stop publishing these tracts because many people were leaving these instead of money, and because waitresses often relied upon tips to help their income, they felt that they were being cheated. This made the Christian appear to be cheap misers, hence making the message ineffective.

The great commission to the church is this:

Go ye therefore, and teach all nations, baptizing them in the name of the Father, and the Son and the Holy Ghost. Teaching them to observe all things, whatsoever I have commanded you. (Matt. 28:19-20)

Go ye into all the world and preach the gospel to every creature. (Mark 16:15)

Chapter Fifteen

What We Don't Know Hurts Us

When I'm teaching my *Apologetics*[23] class, particularly when it comes to defending against cults and other religions, I often say that we cannot possibly defend our faith if we don't know what we believe. I've heard bizarre things among Christians when it comes to things like who Jesus is, the Bible, the Trinity. I've heard quotations that are not even in the Bible as though they were scriptures; hence, it becomes easy for someone to come along and question or even confuse those trying to defend the faith.

Apostle Paul challenged Timothy to study (2 Tim. 2:15). A challenge not just to his young protégé, but to us as well.

[23.] Apologetics—Reasoned arguments or justification of something, typically a theory or religious doctrine to defend doctrine. Branch of theology concerned with the defense or proof of Christianity.

SCOTT A. BRADLEY

Defending Who Jesus Is

Jesus asked his disciples, *"Whom do men say that I am?"* (Matt. 16:13). He did not ask this question because He was concerned with popular opinion or what people necessarily thought of Him, but the questions had a deeper purpose. He was about to reveal Himself to the world as to who he was and His purpose. The responses were respectful, even complimentary: a prophet, one of the prophets of old, great teacher.

Today if you asked what people say about Jesus today, you'd get a variance of answers, but by and large, mostly good (i.e., "Good man, came to show us the way to God, great teacher"). If you asked the major religions today who Jesus was, they'd all say similar things: prophet, messenger, teacher, or reincarnation of an older prophet. Even among the cults, the Jehovah's Witnesses call him a god *created* by God. Originally He was Michael the Archangel. The Mormons say he is the offspring of Father-God along with Lucifer, making them brothers. Although all these are opinions of a *good man*, they still fall short as to who Jesus actually is.

"But whom say ye that I am?" is the question He posed to his disciples. Those who walked close to Him, ate with Him, and saw and heard firsthand the miracles that he performed and sermons that the preached. The response of Peter was deeper than religion. It was greater than what religion could ever do. The response was a revelation inspired

by God Himself. *"Thou art the Christ, the Son of the living God."*

Herein is the difference between religion and the relationship that Christ wants to bring to each individual. Every religion does not believe that Jesus is the Christ. They are opinion based, but not in the true knowledge of who Jesus is. Even within Christianity, there are certain organizations, denominations, and cults that deny this. Jesus said, *"Upon this rock I will build my Church."* The *"Rock"* was not Peter, but the revelation that Peter received from God, "Jesus is the Christ." Although there are many that fall under the religious category of Christianity, not believing that Jesus is the Christ means that they are not a part of the *Church*. Many are religious, belonging to an organization, even acknowledge Jesus one way or another but are not part of the *Church*.

The Historic Jesus

Some of the opinions are less flattering, calling Him things like a mystic, a magician, a false teacher, to denying His existence altogether. However, there are more historic references made to Jesus from non-Christian writings than Julius Caesar. In AD 64, Roman historian Tacitus wrote the following:

> *Nero fasten the guilt… on a class hated for their abominations, called Christians by the populace*

Christus (Christ), from whom the name had its origin.[24]

Reference from Pliny the Younger to the emperor Trajan in AD 112:

They (Christians) were in the habit of meeting on a certain fixed day before it was light, when they sang in alternate verses a hymn of Christ, as to a god, and bound themselves by a solemn oath.[25]

From the writings of the Jewish historian Flavius Josephus:

About this time there lived Jesus, a wise man, if indeed one ought to call him a man. For he... wrought surprising feats...He was the Christ. When Pilate...condemned him to be crucified, those who had come to love him did not give up their affection for him. On the third day he appeared...restored to life.[26]

[24.] Tacitus, Annals 15.44 cited in Strobel, The Case for Christ, p.82

[25.] Pliny, *Letters*, translated by William Melmoth, reviewed by WML Hutchinson (Cambridge: Harvard University Press, 1935) vol. II, cited in Habermas, The Historical Jesus.

[26.] Josephus, Antiquities 18:63-64, cited in Yamauchi, "Jesus Outside the New Testament."

There are many other nonbiblical references made to Jesus proving that He was not a made-up figure but actually existed as a historic person complete with His teachings and working of miracles.

However, there is question as to whether (Jesus) Yeshoushua ben Yousef, a revolutionary at the time of Christ and sometimes confused with Jesus the Messiah, are the same person. (Yeshoushua is the Hebrew name of Jesus derived from Joshua.)

> *Yeshua or Yeshoshua, considered by some to be a Jewish patriot, martyr and the heir to the title "King of the Jews" through the royal line of Galilee. He is seen by others as a revolutionary agitator... there are those who doubt the existence of such a man altogether.*[27]

The Validity of the Bible

The validity of the scriptures is evident as more than 5,800 manuscripts have survived from the early centuries. And although there are no known original surviving complete manuscripts prior to the eleventh century, the comparison of the surviving copies have a variance of one another less than 1%, meaning they have retained what the originals have said. Even the discovery of the Dead Sea

---

[27]. From Wikipedia, the free encyclopedia, User:Scientz / Yehoshua ben Yosef.

scrolls in 1947 that date back to the first century, some dating back to the third century BC, when compare to modern translations have only a overall variance of 1%. The book of Isaiah, which was found intact, was verbatim to modern translations.

> *The Bible, despite textual variations, has been preserved over the centuries with a remarkable degree trustworthy. Though variations exist, the four rules of textual criticism allow us to have a Bible that is very close to what the prophets of Israel and Jesus' followers originally wrote.*[28]

Further, the ancient biblical manuscripts are the oldest surviving manuscripts of any literature. This destroys any myth, particularly by the Islamic religion, that the Bible down through the ages has been tampered with, or by agnostics and atheist that believe the scriptures have been mistranslated. The variances in all cases did not take away from or reinterpret meaning, but were simply differences in spelling, or word arrangements (i.e., Christ Jesus instead of Jesus Christ).[29]

---

[28] David Bowman, "Is Today's Bible the Real Bible?" David Bowman is a graduate student at Grand Rapids Theological Seminary.
[29] Ron Rhodes, "Manuscript Support for Bible's Reality," *Reasoning from the Scriptures,* Rancho Santa Margarita, California.

Defending the Triune God

Although the Trinity is common among Christendom, there are those who do not believe in the triune character of God (i.e., Father, Son, and Holy Spirit). This is because many misinterpret the Trinity to be *three* different Gods, signifying polytheism. However, examination of what the Bible has revealed about God is not polytheism, but one God eternally existent in the three personalities of Father, Son, and Holy Spirit, all of which we see manifested throughout the Bible.

In Islam the idea of a *Trinity* is blasphemous, misinterpreting the concept of three equaling one as three different gods. This misinterpretation is also preached among some Christian circles as well.

Let me first say that there are certain things about the almighty God that are beyond human comprehension, and to try to explain everything about Him is impossible. However, what we do understand is because of the evidence in the Bible. The first mention of God in the Bible is from the Hebrew word Elohim,[30] which describes plural rather than singular. This is not to say plural gods, but plural in personality and purpose. Hence the translation which reveal God as us (i.e., *"Let us make man after our image and our likeness"*).

---

[30] Elohim—Name used frequently for God in the Hebrew Bible. the *-im* denotes plural masculine rather than singular.

As erroneously thought by some, the *Us* would not include angels because the only one that can create life is God. The angels were created. But *Us* as in God eternally existent is three distinct personalities: God the Father, God the Son, and God the Holy Spirit.

The most evident example of the Trinity is at the baptism of Jesus. While the Son is baptized, the Holy Spirit descends upon His shoulder in the form of a dove, and the Father speaks from heaven (Matt. 3:16-17, Mark 1:9-11, Luke 3:21-22, John 1:32).

The triune character is also present in mankind as well for we consist of Body, Soul, and Spirit:

1) **<u>Body</u>**—*the physical portion of man, designed for the passage though time, changes with time, grows old with time, suffers afflictions and pains within time. Will eventually die in time.*

2) **<u>Spirit</u>**—*one of the 2/3 spiritual portion of the individual. The spirit is the personality or character. It is often influenced or developed by the surroundings, environment, culture or upbringing. Child psychologist say that a child personality is usually fully developed by the time the child is three to five years old.*[31] *It is the spirit of a person that can experience emotions,*

---

[31]. Many studies have been done to affirm that once a child has entered the first grade, their personality has already been developed, and they will carry it throughout their life. (Lawrence A. Pervin and Daniel Cervone, *Personality: Theory and Research* (1997).

> *love, hatred, joy, anger, etc all of which can affect the personality in a positive or negative way. The spirit can experience pain, (i.e., heartbreak, spiritual wounds or happiness and joy) (Prov. 18:14).*
> 3) **<u>Soul</u>**—*The eternal conscious state of the individual. The center of intellect, memory, thought process, sense. When Jesus spoke of the rich man who died and went to Hell, he had all of his senses, his memory of his lifetime and recognized Lazarus and Abraham. Every mental and emotional facility that he had in this world he took with him into eternity (Luke 16:19-31).*

There is also the triune dimension of time and space. It is measured by past, present, and future, yet it is always *time*. Or even a piece of *fruit* like an apple, which possesses the core, meat, and skin, but is always an apple. Or *water*, which can be either liquid, gas, or solid, but is always water, and therefore the triune character is common in the universe and in our everyday lives. Yet there are things about the triune God that we cannot understand because He is God of eternity, and although He is the creator of time, not subject to the laws or limitations of time.

Time has a beginning, yet the eternal God has no beginning. He always was, is, and shall be. Time has an ending, but there is no ending to God. He has and will continue to exist throughout eternity.

This concept is impossible to understand or comprehend to those of us limited to the dimensions of time and therefore adds to the mystery and greatness of God.

SCOTT A. BRADLEY

The Reality of Satan: the Enemy of God and Man

When I served in the military, I remember being told, *"The more you know about the enemy, the more of advantage you have over him. The less you know, the more of an advantage he has over you."*

During the time of my service, I spent many times in desert training because of the possible conflicts with the Middle-Eastern nations that were used to fighting in the desert.

It appears that the twenty-first-century church is not conscious of the spirit world, and many Christian do not believe that the devil exists, even some going as far as saying the he is an ancient myth or superstitious belief. It is because of this ignorance that many are falling subject to Satan's tactics and ploys because we fail to recognize that he is the motivator and instigator of everything evil. The spirit-world exists all around us, and even though we don't see them, we see the effects of spirits every day, from wars, murders, thief, blasphemy. In the sexual realm, we see perversion, rapes, incest, abortions, fornication, adultery, pornography, homosexuality, all motivated by the demonic world.

As a youth, I would watch as the church elders cast out demons, hearing them commanding the spirits to "Come out! In Jesus's name!" Sometimes this process took minutes, other times all night, usually with violent convulsion and vomiting. Demons even spoke out of them.

One thing I always noticed was that they couldn't stand the name of Jesus, and it always got an angry or sometimes fearful respond. As I observed, some demons were cast out easier than others, and everyone was not allowed near to minister to the possessed, only the pastor and some of the elders. The reason some were easier to cast out than others, I learned, had to do with the type of spirit, how long they had been in the individual, and the rank of the spirit. Similar to the disciples' attempt to cast the demon out of the epileptic boy, it was not always successful (Mark 9:14-29). But I saw many plagued with such things as alcohol, drugs, and perversions delivered by the power of God as a result of demons cast out of them.

It appears that this rarely happens today. Not because demonic activity has ceased, but because many modern Christians are not spiritual, lack discernment, or don't believe in the existence of the spirit world.

Satan is a fallen spirit (Luke 10:18), defeated by Christ, who has given us power over him. He is not the ruler of hell but will one day be cast into the lake of fire along with all demons as an eternal punishment for their revolt against God in heaven in the dateless past.

While on earth he is a deceiver (Rev. 12:9), accuser (Rev. 12:10) murderer (John 8:44a), the father of lies (John 8:44b), the enemy of both God and man. Because he is a spirit, he does not tire; his goal and strategy has been constant throughout the ages—to take as many souls to hell with him as possible. But Apostle John told us,

Ye are of God, little children, and have overcome them; because greater is He that is in you, than he that is in the world. (1 John 4:4)

Apostle Peter tells us,

Be sober, be vigilant; because your adversary the devil, as a roaring lion, walketh about, seeking whom he may devour. Whom resist steadfast in the faith. (1 Pet. 5:8-9)

Apostle James says,

Submit yourselves therefore to God. Resist the devil, and he will flee from you. (James 4:7)

Though the challenges are great to the twenty-first-century church, we can overcome by holding fast to the word of God uncompromisingly, draw closer to Him through prayer and fasting, and living according to His word and example. Jesus said,

Heaven and earth shall pass away, but my words shall not pass away. (Matt. 24:35)

Chapter Sixteen

America: Blessed and Backslidden

Blessed is the nation whose God is the LORD.
—Psalm 33:12

The wicked shall be turned into hell, and
all of the nations that forgot God.
—Psalm 9:17

America is a blessed nation, a superpower, wealthy, and an example throughout the world. Founded upon Christian principles, it has held to these principles the great majority of her existence. But attitudes in recent decades have slowly turned the nation away from the God of the Bible and has seen an influx of various religions, philosophies, and ideas that have turned the heart of the nation away, even to the point of ridiculing and vilifying those that have held on the Christianity.

When a nation turns from God, it can't help but fall into darkness and see a breakdown of morality, principle, and attitude. One of the reasons for America's fall into ungodly character is because people are afraid to call things wrong for fear of backlash.

Because of God's blessing, America has experienced prosperity beyond any other nation, and although other nations may be religious, they do not necessarily serve the true and living God of the Bible and have not experienced the blessings that God has bestowed upon America.

America is not nor has it ever been perfect. But she is blessed, and many freedom-loving immigrants from all over the world want to come to her blessed shores.

The conclusion is that America is backslidden, like ancient Israel. She has turned her back on God in favor of a self-serving, self-praising arrogance, inviting things into the culture that are contrary to the foundations of its beginning. Just like Israel ignored and rebuffed the prophets of old sent to warn them, so has America rebuffed the true biblical teachings, calling Bible-believing ministers haters, dinosaurs, outdated, crazy, menaces.

The church, when at one time has been the beacon to many, has let the light dim and, its voice, for fear of retribution, silenced.

The Bible says,

> *Let no man deceive you by any means: for that day shall not come, except there come a falling away first. (2 Thess. 2:3)*

That "falling away" is taking place now. The challenge is to the true believers to hold fast to the true gospel, despite the falling away of many. Jesus said, *"Heaven and earth shall pass away, but my words shall never pass away"* (Matt. 24:35).

Men have come and gone, kingdoms have risen and fallen, religions, philosophies. Ideas have all come and gone, and many have failed. But His words are sure, having endured time and test. Therefore, if we stand on His words, we shall stand live forever.

Nevertheless, the foundation of the Lord standeth sure, having this seal, The Lord knoweth them that are his. And let every one that nameth the name of Christ depart from iniquity. (2 Tim. 2:19)

About the Author

Scott A. Bradley is a minister, author, and lecturer. He started preaching at the age of sixteen. By the time he was twenty, he was traveling the length and breadth of America, preaching, teaching, and sharing the gospel education and religious forums as people were blessed by his jubilance and Bible knowledge.

His ministry has also taken him to the foreign countries of England, Nigeria, South Africa, Germany, and Amsterdam. He is a noted lecturer in many national religious conventions with such subjects as Christianity vs. Cultism, Christianity vs. Islam, and the Priesthood of Man and Racial Reconciliation: What should the Church Do?

He has written several books. Most notable are *The Black Man: Cursed or Blessed* in 1993, which received rave reviews, and *Manhood: The Original Priesthood*.

Bradley is also the team chaplain of the Chicago Bulls of the National Basketball Association (NBA) since 1983 and has ministered to many NBA players past and present and had the distinct honor of praying the Lord's Prayer with the team before a national TV audience of 84 million people all over the world after the Bulls won their first NBA championship in 1991.

He holds a bachelor's degree in theological studies from International Apostolic University of Grace and Truth in Dayton, Ohio, and in 1998, the university bestowed upon him an honorary doctorate of divinity for life and ministerial achievements.

Bradley and his wife, Cassandra, have been married over thirty-five years. They have two children and one grandchild.

CPSIA information can be obtained
at www.ICGtesting.com
Printed in the USA
FSHW01n1638240618
49610FS